tees your tot WITHDRAWN

You don't have to be rich or famous to have
the best dressed tot on the block. You won't need to
break the bank or run up your credit card buying
expensive boutique fashions.

You can create your own child's wardrobe by following a few
of the easy steps in this book. You'll learn how
to fuse, embroider, stamp, stencil and embellish simple tees.
We'll show you how to cut, snip and deconstruct a
tee shirt to transform it into a hip fashion statement.
You'll even learn how to dye, batik and
create a sun print on a shirt.

These designs make ideal shower gifts, too. You'll be the
hit of the shower when the mother-to-be asks, "Did
you really make this yourself?" And, if you're
a grandmother, you'll be creating instant
heirlooms for that little tyke.

Check out the 101 designs that follow to get inspired.
Don't forget to consult the "General Instructions"
before you begin your project.
You'll be on your way to building your tot's
unique and special wardrobe, the
best one on
the block.

table of

contents

It takes two to tango–two shirts, that is. They're needed to create this very unusual number. The green sections are cut from one shirt and sewn to the pink one. A lettuce edge is added to the "skirt" and sleeves. The polka dot ribbon was topstitched over the skirt and tied into a crisp bow.

Instructions on page 54

Pink tulle forms a balloon skirt encasing the silk rose petals. Ribbon outlines the tulle and adds interest to the neckline along with the ribbon rose.

Instructions on page 54

Your daughter will be tickled pink when wearing this confection of an outfit. A ruffle of heart print tulle was sewn to the pale pink onesie, then bias tape was stitched over the tulle. Three matching rosebuds finish the design.

Instructions on page 54

Turn this inexpensive tee into a special, one-of-a-kind boutique fashion. Dainty hankies form the diaphanous skirt and a ribbon rose completes the picture. All that's needed—a pair of pink ballet slippers.

Instructions on page 54

Pattern page 59

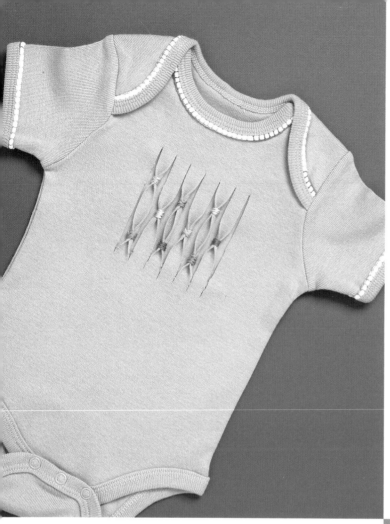

This unique design is destined to elicit lots of comments. The front was cut and then tied in various spots with different colors of embroidery floss. A square of coordinating fabric was added for the backing. Then an interesting stitch was created around the neckline and sleeves.

Instructions on page 54

A triple threat—three shades of pink graduating from light to dark gives this shirt plenty of eye appeal. But that's not all. Check out the lettuce edge around the neckline and bottom edge. Three layers of lettuce edging also decorate the sleeves.

Instructions on page 54
Lettuce edge on page 49

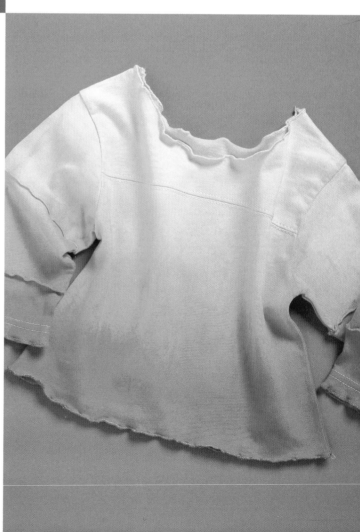

First a white tee-shirt was dyed a luscious shade of pink. Scissors did the rest! The neckline and sleeves were cut off and the bottom, too, transforming the tee into a classy shrug. The tie was formed from the leftover fabric.

Instructions on page 55

Pattern page 60

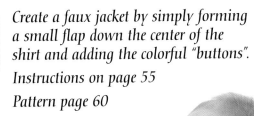

Create a faux jacket by simply forming a small flap down the center of the shirt and adding the colorful "buttons".

Instructions on page 55

Pattern page 60

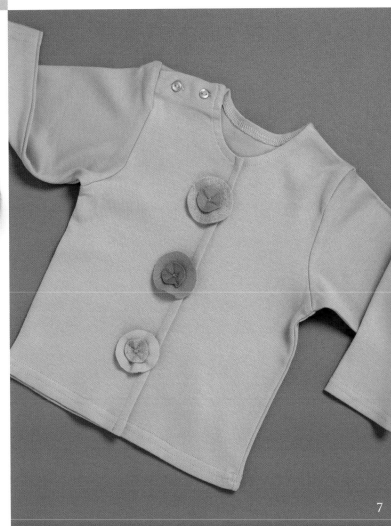

Here's two examples of deconstructed tee-shirts. Simply cut, snip, tie and lace to create these original designs. Buttons can be aligned down the front of the pink laced-up tee for a classic look.

Instructions on page 55

Note

For safety reasons, make sure that any buttons used in your design, are very securely sewn on.

11

Straight from a safari, these animal print fashions will appeal to your world traveler. A combination of ribbon and fabric strips were collaged to the zebra print tee. Furry cuffs completed the picture.

Instructions on page 55

12

Double ruffles of animal print fabric were sewn to the tie-dyed tee.

Instructions on page 55

Fashion a cardigan by simply cutting a tee-shirt down the middle.

Add two coordinating pockets for extra special storage and a lot of pizzazz.

Instructions on page 56

This shirt displays some interesting cutting techniques. Print fabrics become the background—peaking through the cuts.

Instructions on page 56

Pattern page 60

15 An urban design was created first by dyeing the shirt, then cutting it using the diagram. The fringe strips were tied to close the shirt.

Instructions on page 56

16 Trim off the sleeves, create a new neckline and you've transformed a plain tee into a stylish topper.

Instructions on page 56

17

Boys and girls alike will love wearing this Native American-style shirt. The faux suede look was achieved by dyeing the shirt in a solution of coffee. The hems on the sleeves and bottom of the shirt were cut off. Then thin strips (2" x ½" on the sleeves, 2½" x ½" on the bottom) were cut to form fringe. Dimensional paint was used to add the "beads" and color-coordinated trim was glued on using fabric glue.

To coffee dye a shirt:

Add water to your leftover pot of coffee. The less water you use, the darker the shirt will be. We used a 1:1 solution. Soak a damp shirt in the coffee for about 30 minutes. Remove and run under cold water until clear. Heat set.

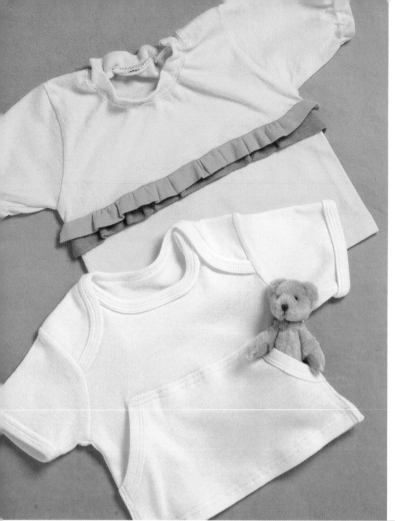

18

Save your tee-shirt scraps and use them to create the double ruffle sewn to this pale yellow shirt. The sleeves and neckline were gathered resulting in a truly feminine edge.

Instructions on page 56

19

Start with a onesie, cut it off at the bottom and turn one side up. Sew along the top and bottom edges leaving the sides open to form one big pocket. How clever is this?

Instructions on page 56

20

Variegated rickrack was sewn to this cut-up tee creating a sassy little shrug—the perfect coverup for the striped onesie.

Instructions on page 56

What an easy way to personalize a onesie. This one was dyed using designer, Connie Rohman's special technique (see page 45), then three hearts were cut right down the center. One heart cut-out was fused to the sleeve of the purple shirt for a coordinated effect.

Cutting pattern page 60

22

Patches of vintage fabrics were pieced together to form a gathered skirt and transformed this bright red tee into a darling dress.

Instructions on page 57

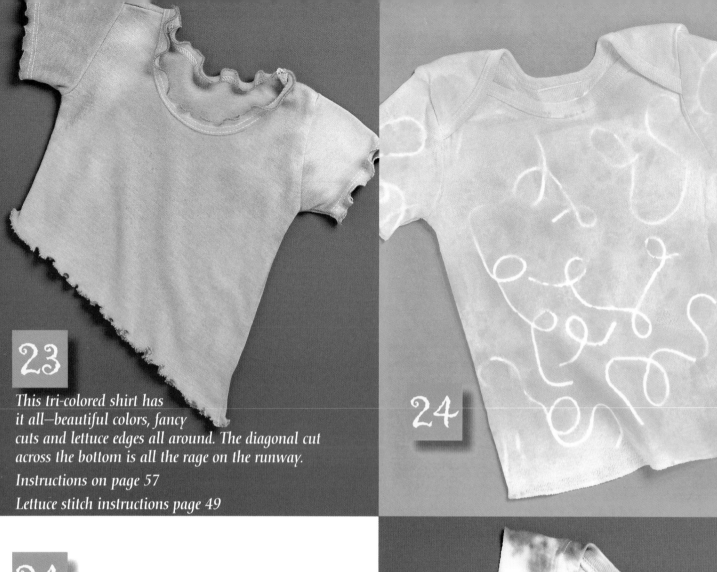

23

This tri-colored shirt has it all—beautiful colors, fancy cuts and lettuce edges all around. The diagonal cut across the bottom is all the rage on the runway.

Instructions on page 57

Lettuce stitch instructions page 49

24

Believe it or not—the design on this cool shirt was created using spaghetti! Cooked pasta creates the wiggly design and fabric spray paint provides the color. Presto! you've got yourself a one-of-a-kind design.

Instructions on page 53

25

Tuck a small stuffed toy in his pocket and he'll never want to take this shirt off. The bold tie-dyed colors make this shirt a stand out. The sleeveless look is created by merely cutting off the existing sleeves and guess what? One sleeve becomes the pocket. Leave the hem on the cut-off sleeve to save you work, then sew on the pocket.

Instructions on page 57

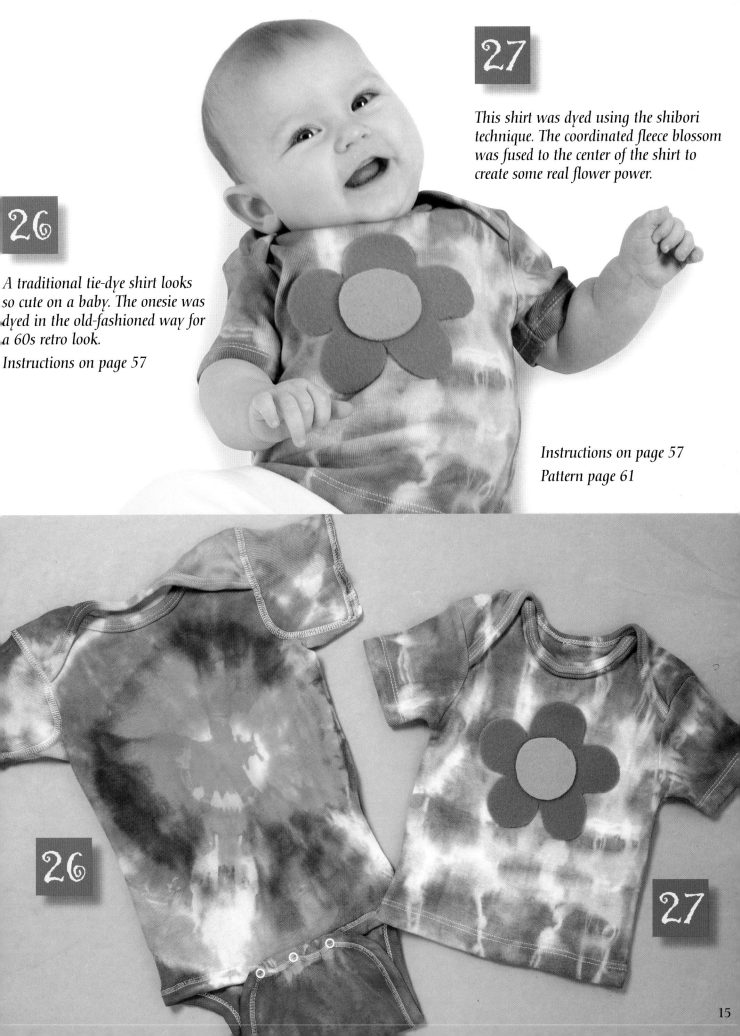

27

This shirt was dyed using the shibori technique. The coordinated fleece blossom was fused to the center of the shirt to create some real flower power.

26

A traditional tie-dye shirt looks so cute on a baby. The onesie was dyed in the old-fashioned way for a 60s retro look.

Instructions on page 57

Instructions on page 57
Pattern page 61

26

27

28

Pretty posies are quick to stitch on this lavender tee.

Pattern on page 61

Stitch instructions on page 51

29

Stitched lazy daisies top the ribbo stems. The narrow ribbons were attached using fabric glue.

Pattern on page 61

Stitch instructions on page 51

This shirt was first dyed red, then "Little Love" was stitched around the tiny heart.

Pattern on page 62

Stitch instructions on page 51

30

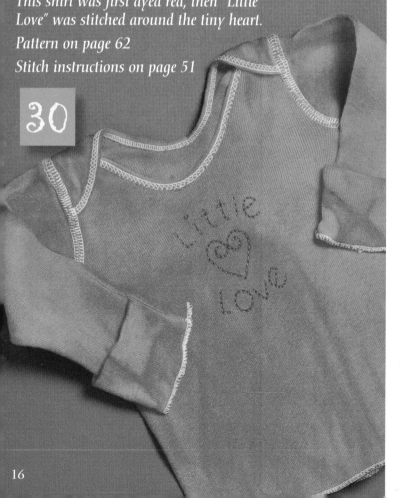

33

31

A souvenir of Paris for baby? Why not?

Pattern on page 62

Stitch instruction page 51

32

A stylish balloon skirt was stitched to a lavender tee. Then the little dress was embellished with a French poodle.

Sewing instructions page 49
  (Adding skirts or ruffles)

Pattern page 62

Stitch instructions on page 51

33

Any little princess will love this tee, stitched especially for her. Tiny stars stitched with silver thread add sparkle.

Pattern on page 62

Stitch instructions on page 51

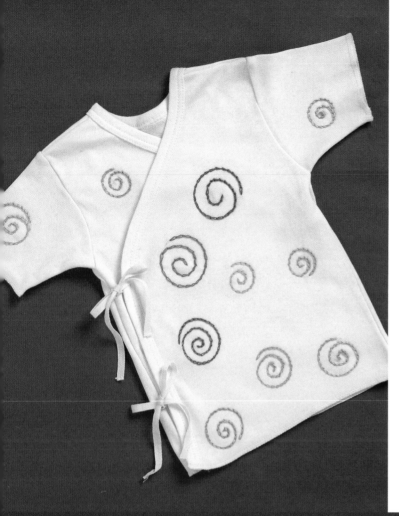

Chain-stitched swirls embellish this kimono-style tee.

Patterns are on page 64

Stitch instructions page 51

Mary will surely want this little lamb, and a young maestro will declare his passion for music quite early wearing this musical tee.

Patterns on pages 63

Stitch instructions on page 51

A romantic heart decorates this light pink shirt, while a Parisian kitty cat graces the bright pink tee.

Patterns on page 63
Stitch instructions on page 51

37

38

39

The pink striped tee is the perfect background for the "Kiss Me" design.

Pattern on page 64
Stitch instructions on page 51

Tip

Remember to always think of the baby's comfort. If there are several embroidered knots on the inside of the shirt, you might want to fuse a piece of soft flannel or fleece to cover them.

Designer, Connie Rohman dyed this onesie using her immersion dye technique (see page 45). Then a handsome little snail was embroidered as a finishing touch.

Dyeing instructions on page 45

Pattern on page 64

Stitch instructions page 51

An oversized rose was stitched using al.
French knots on this red turtleneck onesie

Pattern on page 64

Stitch instructions on page 51

41

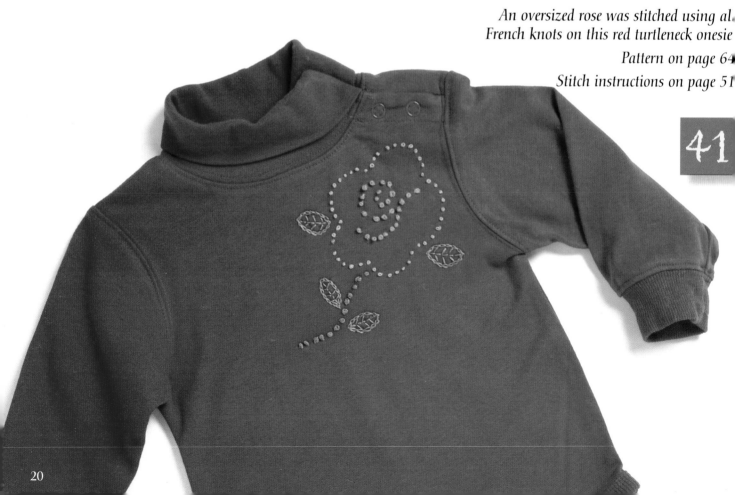

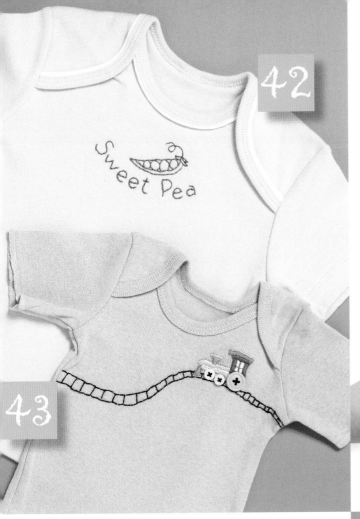

42

43

The train and "Sweet Pea" designs were each embroidered to baby tees. Buttons were added to the train for wheels.

Patterns on pages 64 and 65

Stitch instructions
page 51

44

Three techniques created this cute little tee—dyeing, fusing and stitching. The flowers were cut from print fabric. Try your hand at free-style embroidery and add accents to the fabric. We added stitched petals around the flowers and French knots to the centers.

Instructions on page 57

Stitch instructions on page 51

The Ooo LaLa shirt and scroll heart
can both be embroidered in a snap.

Patterns on pages 65

Stitch instructions on page 51

The neckline and sleeves were trimmed off,
then a lettuce edge finished the raw edges.
Lavender curlicues were embroidered for an
elegant touch. It tops a yellow-striped shirt
for a fashionable, layered look.

Pattern on page 66

Lettuce stitch instructions page 49

Stitch instructions page 51

48

49

A lime green tee was lovingly stitched with colorful lazy daisies while the blue onesie was stitched with a word that needs no translation.

Patterns on pages 66 and 67

Stitch instructions page 51

bebé

50

This cute little chick is a fabric appliqué. Embroider the long legs following the pattern.

Pattern on page 67

Fusing instructions on page 50

51

This busy bee shirt is another example of fabric appliqué and embroidery.

Patterns are on page 68

Stitch instructions page 51

Fusing instructions page 50

52

Glub, glub. This
underwater design is
for the future diver.

Instructions on page 57

Stitch instructions page 51

Fusing instructions page 50

Pattern page 67

53

One cut down the center and voila!, you've
got a darling little cardigan. Add the
beautiful butterfly appliqué and you've got a
one-of-a-kind tee that will get rave reviews.

Pattern on page 69

Stitch instructions page 51

Cutting instructions page 49
 (to find center of shirt)

Fusing instructions page 50

54

Star bright, star light. Fleece stars emblazon this long sleeved onesie. Ties of embroidery floss accent each star.

Pattern on page 69

55

Round and round we go. Circles of pretty purples, blues and green add a folk art element to the lavender onesie.

Patterns on page 69

Stitch instructions page 51

56

All little boys love dinosaurs. Create this polka dot version for your own reptile lover.

Pattern on page 69

Fusing instructions page 50

57

For the aspiring pilot, add an airplane design flying in the clouds.

Pattern on page 70

Fusing instructions page 50

58

The gingham pup
and kitty cat are both
examples of fabric
appliqués. Stitch their
eyes and the cat's
whiskers following the
patterns using black
floss. Then add the cat's
tail with decorative yarn.

Patterns on page 70

Fusing instructions
on page 50

Stitching instructions
on page 51

59

60

A western style tee was created by adding a denim star, topped with the leather label from a pair of levis. As an alternative, use a square of faux leather fabric for the patch.

Pattern on page 69

Fusing instructions page 50

61

Patterns on pages 71 and 72
Fusing instructions on page 50

62

He'll have his own car on a tee-shirt designed exclusively for him. If he's ready to fly into the wild blue yonder, this airplane design is thumbs up. The rickrack was easily added to the appliqué design using fabric glue.

PUBLIC LIBRARY
DANVILLE, ILLINOIS

63

Sweets for the sweet. The cherry topped cupcake was finished with embroidered details.

Pattern on page 71

Stitch instructions on page 51

64

A trio of hearts displays a sampler of fabric prints.

Pattern on page 75

Fusing instructions on page 50

This fused heart design was accented with dashes of red dimensional paint. What could be easier?

Fusing instructions on page 50

Pattern on page 75

65

66

67

Colorful fabric appliqués decorate
these crisp white tees. Both were
accented with creative stitching.

Patterns on pages 73 and 74

Stitch instructions on page 51

Fusing instructions on page 50

How clever! Fuse a fabric heart to the center of a blue tee, trim off the existing sleeves and replace them with cap sleeves of matching fabric.

Pattern on page 74

Instructions on page 58

Fusing instructions page 50

70

69

Paisleys were cut from a bandanna and fused to a bright red shirt. Add some French knots, referring to the photo, to decorate and you've got a very stylish tee. Don't forget the sleeve.

Fusing instructions page 5(

Stitch instructions page 51

70

Butterflies flit over this blue onesie. Fuse them on and then add details with a minimum of embroidery stitches.

Patterns on page 76

Stitch instructions page 51

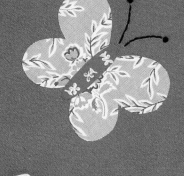

71

Create this floral decoration using fabrics of primary colors. Add the stem using a simple embroidery stitch.

Patterns on page 75

Fusing instructions page 50

Stitch instructions page 51

A budding soccer star will wear this tee to all the games. Fused squares of brightly colored fabrics were topped with an iron-on appliqué. If you can't find this appliqué, make your own using the pattern on page 76. Either fuse fabric pieces to create the ball or embroider it.

Pattern on page 76

Fusing instructions page 50

Sock monkeys are all the rage. Why not add one to your child's shirt? These two examples both were appliquéd using the traditional Red Heal sock. Facial features were added using fleece pieces and buttons.

74

73

Patterns on page 76
Fusing instructions on page 50

75

Your tiny astronomer will love this navy tee sporting celestial designs.

Patterns on page 75

Fusing instructions page 50

76

Kids will love having shirts displaying their animal friends. The fun elephant sports a pair of big ears which were sewn to the face and left partially loose for a floppy effect. The cute puppy with plaid ears is ever so huggable.

77

Patterns on pages 77 and 78

Fusing instructions page 50

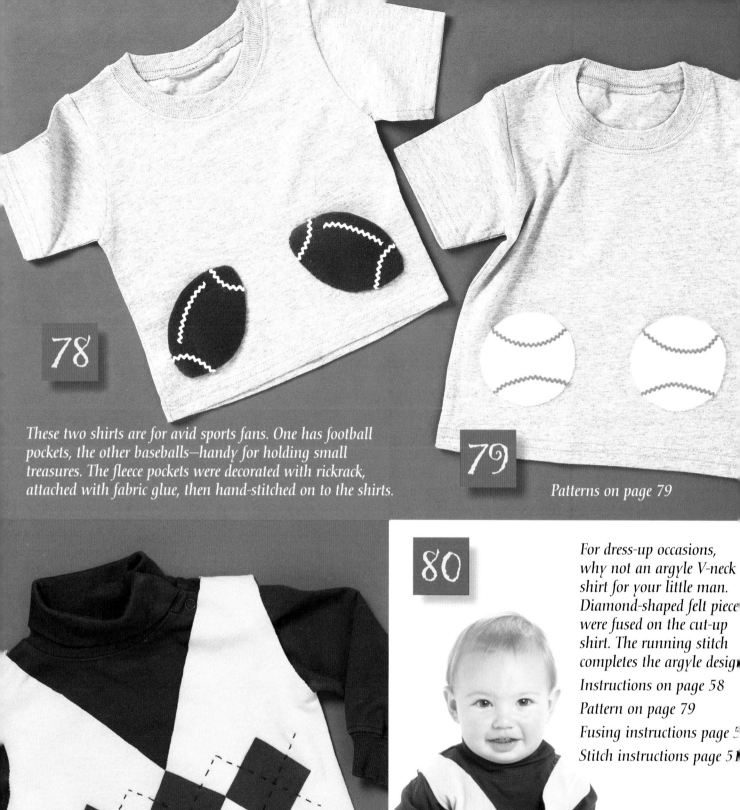

78

79

These two shirts are for avid sports fans. One has football pockets, the other baseballs—handy for holding small treasures. The fleece pockets were decorated with rickrack, attached with fabric glue, then hand-stitched on to the shirts.

Patterns on page 79

80

For dress-up occasions, why not an argyle V-neck shirt for your little man. Diamond-shaped felt piece were fused on the cut-up shirt. The running stitch completes the argyle design

Instructions on page 58

Pattern on page 79

Fusing instructions page 5

Stitch instructions page 5

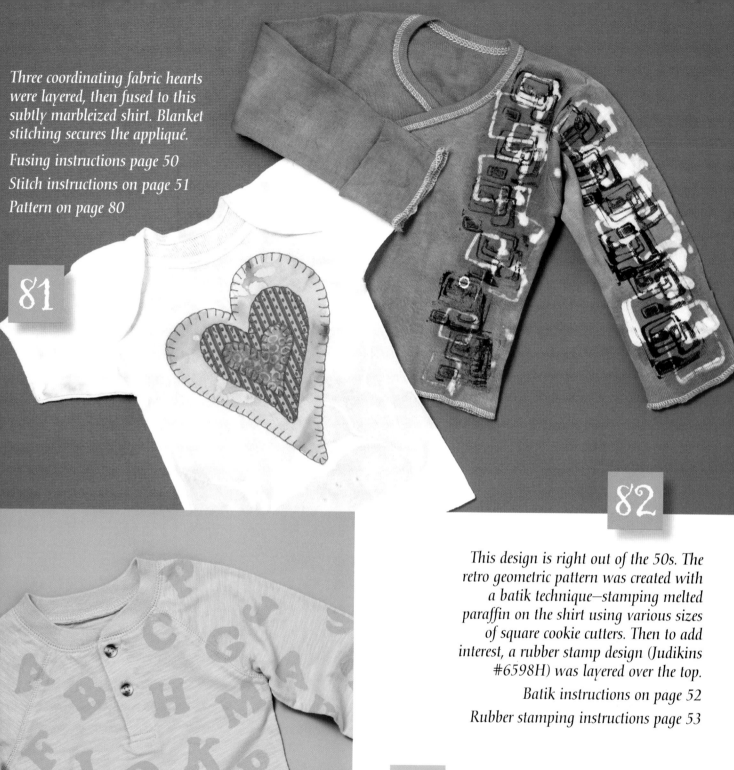

Three coordinating fabric hearts were layered, then fused to this subtly marbleized shirt. Blanket stitching secures the appliqué.

Fusing instructions page 50
Stitch instructions on page 51
Pattern on page 80

81

82

This design is right out of the 50s. The retro geometric pattern was created with a batik technique—stamping melted paraffin on the shirt using various sizes of square cookie cutters. Then to add interest, a rubber stamp design (Judikins #6598H) was layered over the top.

Batik instructions on page 52
Rubber stamping instructions page 53

83

Early learning can't hurt. Your little tot will be way ahead of the curve when he wears his alphabet on his shirt. Bold, oversized letters were stamped (Crafty Productions foam stamps) randomly to this onesie to make future spelling a snap.

Rubber stamping instructions on page 53

84

How easy to transform a plain tee into a designer special. Simply stamp down one side with Op Art patterns (Hot Potatoes #J458 and 460, and Judikins #6598H) in bright colors. The result—a shirt your future skateboarder will love.

Stamping instructions page 53

Both of these designs were created using paintsticks, a kind of crayon for grownups. This is a fun technique and best of all doesn't change the feel of the fabric. The nautical design is finished with a blanket stitch around the neckline, sleeves and bottom edge.

Instructions on page 53

87

Instructions on page 53

88

Nature lovers will enjoy these sun print designs. Sometimes your plan doesn't work, but the result can still be interesting as in the shirt on the left. Instructions were followed—but the design didn't appear. Oops. But we liked the tie-dye, velvety look that resulted. The shirt on the right was a success.

89

After dyeing this onesie, add the stamped design "ROCK STAR BABY" (Ransom Alphabet by Plaid #4283L). Is a concert tour in his future?

Instructions on page 58

Fit for an empress. Rectangles of exotic fabrics were first fused and then sewn to this rust colored shirt. The Chinese calligraphy was stenciled down the center, and to complete the design, a handsome braided frog was sewn to front.

Fusing instructions on page 50

Stenciling instructions on page 52

91

Stylized glyphs of earth tones were stamped on this bright orange onesie suitable for a future archeologist.

Rubber stamping instructions on page 53

Cut a black tee up the front and you've got a cardigan. Add some colorful rickrack and you've got a jacket fit for a fashionista.

Instructions on page 58

The white kimono and pant set were transformed into an Asian-inspired design. Chinese frogs were tacked along the opening and red baby rickrack was applied all around using fabric glue.

94

Fun in the sun is the theme for this shirt. The palm tree and sun are simply fused to the shirt, followed by the rickrack. Refer to this photo for design placement, then use fabric glue to apply the rickrack.

93

tttern on page 80
ising instructions
ι page 50

41

Designer Gallery

We asked six very talented artists to contribute a baby tee-shirt for this book. We were hoping to receive a variety of designs and techniques that were unique and original. And we weren't disappointed.

Each design should serve as an inspiration for you to try your own tee-shirt. Examine these designer's samples and use them as a springboard to develop your distinctive style. Hopefully, you'll be inspired enough to create a one-of-a-kind boutique original for your little one.

Claudine Helmuth

Claudine Helmuth is an internationally known collage artist. Her work has been featured in numerous magazines, used as book and CD illustrations, licensed as greeting cards, journals, gift product and more.

In addition to creating her artwork full time, Claudine teaches mixed media workshops.

She has written two best selling boo - Collage Discovery Workshop and Collage Discovery Workshop: Beyon the Unexpected.

She and her husband, Paul make th home in Orlando, Fl. along with th spoiled fur kids: Toby the Wonder D and Mable and Maggie, the cats.

www.collageartist.com

"Into each life some rain must fall". Claudine used bright and fun applic flowers and a puffy cloud to illustra this theme. Dainty embroidery stitch help paint the picture.

95

Jane LaFazio

96

Whether fabric, paper or canvas, mixed media artist, Jane La Fazio displays a common theme of texture and color in her works. When she's not traveling, Jane is teaching classes and working on her various projects. She makes her home in San Diego, California.

www.PlainJaneStudio.com

Jane designed this unique ensemble. A subtle tie dye effect was achieved by bunching up sections of the fabric and securing with rubber bands then dyeing in a coffee bath. Jane then cut her own stamp and applied the exotic swirl design. Detail was created with a running stitch accenting the design and edging the shirt and pants. A real labor of love.

97

Connie Rohman

Connie Rohman dyes her own fabric and works with reverse appliqué as well as other techniques. She uses the traditional materials and methods of quilt making to explore abstract shape, line and color. Connie has won numerous awards for her art quilts.

e-mail: crohman1@yahoo.com

Connie used her immersion dye techniques to create these three fabulous tees.

Connie Rohman's Dyeing Technique

Connie prefers using Procion Dyes because the colors are rich and saturated. She usually uses primary colors (red, yellow and blue) and mixes them to get the color that she wants. But she says you can purchase the dye colors pre-mixed and ready to use. This is especially handy when you're working with small projects such as baby tee-shirts.

She rarely tests the dye bath because she likes to be surprised with the color. But, if you want to test the color, you can dip a piece of paper towel in the solution to get an idea of what color the dye will be. This isn't always foolproof, however. But Connie says,"with practice and keeping notes, you can learn to get within the range of color you want."

"Don't be afraid to experiment with dyes," Connie says. You can use pieces of tee-shirts or shirts you find at thrift shops or garage sales to experiment with. Connie stresses that you should always wash your thrift shop shirts before putting them in the dye solution. This removes any sizing from the shirt and will give you a more accurate color.

To dye the shirt:

You'll need:

2 colors of Procion dyes
Table salt
Sodium carbonate
Water
Bowls or tubs
Protective gloves
Baggies

1. Prepare the dye according to the package directions.

2. Stuff the shirt in a small plastic bag and pour the dye over the top.

3. Massage the bag 2 or 3 times during the first hour of dyeing.

4. Leave in the dye overnight.

5. Rinse until water runs clear. Hang to dry.

6. For the second color (over-dyeing) pour a little less of the second dye in another baggie (this way some of the first dye color stays put) and scrunch the shirt in.

7. Leave in bag overnight. Rinse until water runs clear. Hang to dry.

Note: To achieve the interesting over dyed effect, you can first dye the shirt in a blue dye, then with red and you get a purple shirt with red and blue tones in it. Or, if you start with yellow, then blue, you'll get a lovely green.

Connie keeps a bin of what she calls "ugly" fabrics. At the end of a dyeing session she throws some of these ugly fabrics into left over dyes just to see what happens. She's sometimes pleasantly surprised with the results. She says, "what do you have to lose, the dye was going to get washed down the drain, so why not see what it does."

And finally, Connie says, "have fun experimenting with dyes. You'll be surprised with all the beautiful and unique baby tee-shirts you can create yourself."

98

Elin received her MFA in costume design and worked as a wardrobe stylist in film and television. Her experience in building costumes, painting, dyeing and manipulating fabrics evolved into quilt making. Elin's award-winning art quilts are in many public a private collections and have been exhibited in numerous art galleries. She lives with her husband in South Sale New York.

www.elinwaterston.com

Elin Waterston contributed this lovely tee-shirt which started out as a plain white onesie. She hand dyed it orange, then block printed four red-orange flowers on t front. She then appliquéd th bird which was block printe on blue fabric by machine stitching it in place. The fin step was free motion stitchir all around the bird.

Sandra Pearson

Sandra majored in art and first taught art to elementary school students. She has dabbled in oil painting, fabric arts and photography. Her creations have merged her passion for the arts and family. She currently resides in Norwich, Connecticut.

Sandra scanned her grandchild's artwork, then printed the design on an inkjet fabric sheet. She layered the design with other fabrics and then sewed it to this turtleneck onesie.

How about an aprés ski number to wear at a favorite mountain resort? Sandra used a sea sponge to add color to white fabric. She then stamped snowflakes using white paint. The fabric was fused to the shirt and sewn on for good measure.

Another wintertime tog is this cute snowman shirt. The fabric was decorated the same as above. Then the snowman design was stamped over the top using various Jacquard paints. Again it was fused to the shirt and topstitched to secure.

100

Anita Byers

Anita Byers is a featured designer for Stampington Magazine and Somerset Studio. She strongly believes that her interest in artistic exploration was responsible for her recovery from cancer. Anita and her husband, Tom, make their home in Huntington Beach, California.

Anita contributed these three original designs. Using a tattoo-themed fabric print, she fused different elements of the print on the onesie.

Three sock monkeys were cut out of print fabric and fused to the kimono-style shirt. Bright red rickrack accents the sleeves and neckline and continues down the front.

Any little boy would love this aviation-inspired onesie. The fabric airplane was cut out and fused to a background of blue print fabric. "fly" was stamped using alphabet stamps and the design was then fused to the shirt and edged with lime green rickrack.

101

General Instructions

Supplies you may need:

Fabric scissors
Small sharp scissors
Tracing paper
Transfer paper (graphite paper)
Transfer pencil
Pins
Needle and thread
Sewing machine
Embroidery hoop
Iron

Preparing Garments

Most washable garments should be washed, dried and pressed before starting your project. This preshrinks the fabric and also removes any sizing which may prevent paints and fusible webbing from adhering properly. Do not use fabric softener.

Using Patterns

Included in this book are patterns for cutting fabric appliqué shapes or for use as placement guides. You may copy the patterns either with tracing paper and pencil or by photocopying. If the pattern shows only half the design, fold the tracing paper or photocopy on the dotted line to get the entire design when you open the paper.

Pin your photocopy or tracing to the fabric.

Transferring patterns to fabric

If you're going to transfer the design to the fabric, choose one of the following techniques that best suits the project:

- Fabric marking pen with disappearing ink: Allows you to place a tracing underneath a light-colored or sheer garment and draw over the pattern lines that show through the fabric. After tracing, the marks will eventually fade away.

- Graphite paper (or transfer paper): Graphite paper is available in a variety of colors so you can choose the one that will best show up on your garment. Determine the placement of your design, hold or pin the tracing in place on one side and slide the graphite paper under it, colored side down; redraw the pattern lines on the tracing paper, and they will be reproduced on the garment.

3. Transfer pencil: Use to transfer detailing after the pattern has been traced onto tracing paper with a regular pencil. Turn the tracing over and use the transfer pencil to redraw the pattern lines where they show through to the back of the tracing paper. This makes the design an iron-on transfer; when you turn it over onto the fabric and press it in place with an iron, the lines will appear on the garment.

To Find the Center of a shirt

Fold the tee-shirt in half matching the side seams and shoulder seams. Use an iron to press down the fold. Open and the fold line will mark the center. Use this line either for marking the center of the shirt or as a guide for cutting the shirt up the front.

To add a skirt or ruffle to shirts

1. To determine fabric size, measure the circumference of the bottom of the shirt. (Slightly stretch the shirt as you measure.) Double the measurement and cut a strip of fabric to that length. Cut the fabric the desired width, adding 1".

2. With right sides facing, sew the short ends together using ¼" seam allowance forming a circle.

3. Machine hem one long side of the strip turning the edge under ¼" and then another ¼".

4. To gather the ruffle, sew a running stitch ¼" down from the edge of the non-hemmed side. Pull the threads to gather the fabric to fit the bottom of the shirt, stretching the shirt bottom.

5. With right sides together and edges matching, pin the ruffle to the bottom of the shirt starting with the seam of the ruffle positioned center back. Stretch the bottom of the shirt as you go.

6. Sew the ruffle onto the shirt using ½" seam allowance. Trim.

Balloon Skirt

1. To determine fabric size: Measure the circumference of the bottom of the shirt (slightly stretch the shirt as you measure). Double the measurement for the length. For the width of the skirt, double the size desired, adding ½". Cut a strip of fabric to the those measurements.

2. With right sides facing, sew the short ends of the strip together using ¼"seam allowance.

3. Fold the strip in half with wrong sides facing. Sew a running stitch ¼" down from the edge. Pull the threads to gather the fabric to fit the bottom of the shirt, stretching the shirt bottom.

4. To finish, follow instructions 5 and 6 from "adding skirt or ruffle".

Lettuce edges

1. To give the neckline, sleeve and bottom edge of the tee a ruffled look ("lettuce" edge), first cut off the ribbing and existing hem. You can use a contrasting color of thread or one that matches the shirt.

2. Press the fabric edges under for a hemline.

3. Set the machine for the shortest zigzag stitch. Use an embroidery or satin-stitch presser foot.

4. Holding the fabric in front of and behind the presser foot, stretch as you zigzag along the creased edge letting the needle fall off the edge of the fold on the right-hand swing. Stretch the fabric by pulling it taut as you stitch for maximum ruffling.

5. On the wrong side, trim the hem allowance close to the stitching.

Note: For different effects, try lettuce edging the edges without turning them under, or lettuce edge the ribbing.

General Instructions

Applying Appliqués

To attach fabric appliqués and other embellishments to garments, you may choose fusing or hand–stitching techniques. Practice with the different techniques so you can discover the differences and advantages of each.

Fusing gives a smooth, regular appearance to fabric appliqués attached to garments; in most cases it is the preferred method of adhering appliqués. Fusing or hand–stitching is better on lightweight materials. Hand–stitching can give a more finished edge and is desirable when attaching only the edges of appliqués. Some materials work better with glue, especially for adding lace, trims, cords, and sequins.

About Fusing

Fusible webbing is a heat–set adhesive made into sheets that are covered with paper on both sides. This webbing allows you to add adhesives to your fabric, which enables you to iron the fabric to another piece of fabric. Some fusible webbings are Heat N Bond®, Wonder Under® and Steam–A–Seam2®. Follow the individual manufacturer's directions supplied with the webbing you decide to use.

In this book we have used Steam–A–Seam2. We like this fusible web because once you have the web on your fabric and before ironing it, you can stick it to your project and reposition the appliqué until you're happy with the placement. Then, when you're ready, you iron it to your garment.

We've given directions for fusing where you actually place the Steam–A–Seam over your pattern and trace onto the paper liner. This eliminates the step of tracing the appliqué pattern onto tracing paper.

Fusing using Steam–A–Seam2®

1. Before you begin, you'll need to determine the proper side of the Steam–A–Seam to trace your pattern. To do this, peel back one corner slightly. See which side has the webbing (sticky side) and mark that side with an "X". Do not peel off any of the liner paper yet.

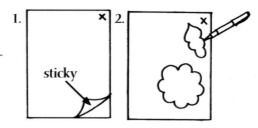

2. Place the sheet of Steam–A–Seam ("X"–side up) over the pattern. Trace your appliqué designs directly onto the sheet of Steam–A–Seam. (Reverse pattern if necessary.)

Tip: Mark the color on each piece referring to the pattern.

3. Roughly cut around each piece.

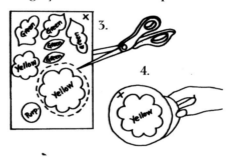

4. Peel off the bottom liner paper. Now you'll have the liner paper with the sticky side. Stick this to the wrong side of the fabric pieces.

5. With a pressing cloth on top, use a steam iron to iron the piece to the fabric.

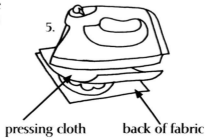

pressing cloth   back of fabric

6. Cut out around your traced line

7. Peel off the remaining liner pap Now you'll have a cut-out fabri piece that is sticky on the back.

8. At this point you can stick the appliqués to your garment and arrange the pieces until you are happy with the design. Then go on to Step 9.

9. With pressing cloth on top and your appliqué sticky–side down use steam iron to iron the piece to your garment.

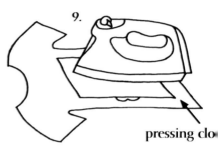

pressing clo

Once you've ironed the appliqués your garment, you can either cho to stitch around the design or just leave as is. See embroidery stitche on page 51.

Embroidery

Use an embroidery needle (sharp-pointed) for stitching. Floss is composed of six strands, use one to three strands, depending on the project instructions. Cut the floss i 18" lengths. It is best to pre-wash floss before using to remove any excess dye, especially colors such as red and black. An embroidery hoop should be used to hold fabri taut when stitching. However, whe stitching on heavy fabric, you wou need an embroidery hoop. Follow the diagrams provided on page 51 for each stitch to see just how it is formed. To begin, secure the floss the back of the fabric with a small knot.

Embroidery Stitches

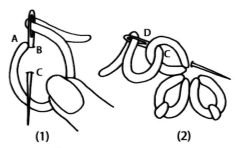 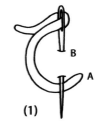 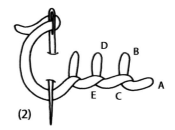

(1)   (2)

Lazy daisy stitch
(1) Bring needle up at A (center of the "daisy"); make a loop with thread and hold down. Go in at B, next to A, and come out again at C. Draw needle and thread over loop and tie down with tiny stitch at D.

Blanket stitch
(1) Come up at A; go in at B, leaving a small loop. Come up again at C directly below B and in line with A while holding thread under needle with thumb. Pull thread through.
(2) Repeat.

 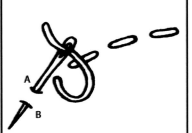 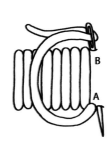 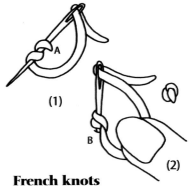

(1)

(2)

Chain stitch

Bring the floss out at the top of the line and hold down with left thumb. Insert the needle where it last emerged and bring the point out a short distance away. Pull the floss through, keeping the working floss under the needle point.

Running Stitch

Go in at A and out at B, making the upper stitches of equal length. The under stitches should also be of equal length, but half the size or less of the upper stitches.

Satin stitch

Come up at A; go in at B. Come up again very close to A and go in close to B, keeping the stitches even and smooth.

French knots

(1) Come up at A. Hold needle close to fabric and coil thread snugly around needle two or three times.

(2) Insert needle at B, very close to A but not in the same hole, meanwhile keeping thread taut with fingers of free hand. More precise but smaller knots can be made by coiling the thread only once around the needle.

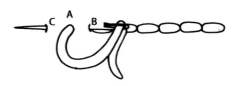 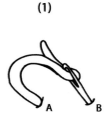 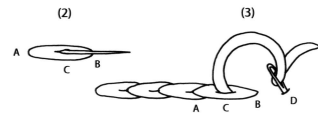

(1)   (2)   (3)

Backstitch

Come up at A; go in at B; come up again at C. Repeat, going back into same hole at A as the last stitch. Keep stitches uniform in size.

Split stitch
(1) Come up at A; go in at B.

(2) Come up at C piercing through center of stitch, splitting it in the middle.

(3) Needle goes in at D, a little ahead of B. Repeat to end of row.

General Instructions

Transferring Photos Onto Fabric

Use your computer printer to transfer photos to fabric. Inkjet printable fabric is available in craft, fabric and quilt stores. The fabric has a paper backing that can be run through your computer inkjet printer. An image of your choice can be printed on the fabric, then incorporated into your tee–shirt design. You can scan clip art, photos or illustrations. Also, use your computer to create text. Just put it through your inkjet printer as if it's a piece of paper.

Dyeing Instructions

Dyeing your own fabric is such a fun way to express yourself and to create your very own textile designs. You'll be surprised at the variety of designs you can come up with.

Since we dealt with such small projects in this book, we felt that simple dyeing methods would be best. We tried to use products that are readily available either from your local grocery or craft store. These are the two main dyes we used:

Rit Dye: This is probably the easiest to find fabric dye. It's sold in grocery stores, craft stores and discount stores among others. It's easy to use, too. Follow the instructions on the package for best results.

Dylon Permanent Fabric Dye: This dye works well on all natural and polyester/cotton fabrics. It's easy to use and provides a nice vibrant color.

All dyed projects should be pre-washed. Prepare the dyes according to the package instructions. Wet the shirt before applying dye or soaking in the dye. Use protective gloves when dyeing fabrics.

Batik

Batik literally means "wax written". It is a way of decorating fabric by covering part of it with a coat of wax and then dyeing the fabric. The waxed area keeps its original color and when the wax is removed the contrast between the dyed and undyed area makes the pattern.

For best results use 100% cotton fabrics and cold water dye for this technique. You will need paraffin wax which is readily available in grocery stores. For the design on page 37, we used different sizes of square cookie cutters – 1", 2" and 3".

1. Melt the paraffin in a double boiler.

2. Carefully dip the edge of a cookie cutter or rubber stamp into the wax and stamp on the shirt. Continue dipping and stamping to complete the design.

3. When you're finished stamping with wax, wet the shirt and submerge it into the cold dye. Let soak for about 30 minutes. Remove and run COLD water over the shirt until the water runs clear. Hang to dry.

4. Place paper towels over the shirt and iron over the design. This will melt the excess wax from the shirt. Continue to iron until all wax is removed.

5. If desired, stamp a design over the top of the batik design using a rubber stamp and fabric paint (see shirt on page 37).

Stenciling

1. Tape the stencil to the shirt using masking tape on corners. Apply paint to a stencil brush and then dab the brush on a paper towel so that the brush is almost dry.

2. Hold brush vertically and use either a dabbing of swirling motion. Start at the edges of the stencil while you have more paint on your brush and let it get lighter (less paint) towards the center. This will give you a shaded effect.

3. When finished painting, carefully peel away the stencil. Let the paint dry, then iron the design to heat set.

Using Dimensional Fabric Paint

Fused or glued appliqués have raw edges. One way to keep the fabric from fraying and to stop the appliqué from coming off the garment is to apply dimensional fabric paint around the edges. This paint comes in a plastic applicator bottle with a fine tip. It's available in dozens of colors and finishes. For the paint to flow freely, it is best to store the bottles upside down (an egg carton makes a handy container). If the paint is clogged when you open it, insert a straight pin into the tip.

Correct paint mistakes by sliding a sharp knife between the paint and the fabric and lifting off the paint: remove excess paint smears with non–acetone nail polish remover. If this isn't possible, add to the design to incorporate the mistake, making it look as if it were intentional. After you completely outline all the appliqué, lay the garment flat on your work surface and allow the paint to dry.

Using Acrylic Fabric Paint

Before painting, hand–wash your garment or wash it on the gentle cycle in hot water. This removes sizing. Hang or lay the garment flat to dry (don't use a dryer). Iron it if it has gotten wrinkled. After painting, heat set by pressing with a dry iron. Always use a pressing cloth.

Washing Your Embellished Garments

Generally, garments with embellishments glued or fused on or with paint added should be turned inside out for washing. Wash by hand or machine, following the garment manufacturer's guidelines. Allow to dry flat or on a line rather than in the dryer. A garment stamped with acrylic paint can be washed by hand or on the gentle cycle of your machine. Wait about 72 hours after painting before the first washing. Turn the garment inside out and use warm or cool water and mild detergent. Tumble dry on medium heat or lay it flat to dry.

Caution: Bowls or containers that are used for dyeing should not be used for food.

General Instructions

Rubber Stamping with Paint

In this book we have used acrylic paints for rubber stamping on garments. Practice your stamping with paints before stamping on your garment. Use a paper towel or scrap piece of fabric to practice. When you start stamping on your garment, apply the paint to your stamp using a foam brush, then stamp on a paper towel to remove any excess paint. You'll need to reapply paint every 3 or 4 stamp applications.

Pasta Printed Fabric

You'll need:
Pasta (we used spaghetti)
Spray fabric paint (2 or 3 colors)
Shirt

Cook the spaghetti. Place the wet spaghetti on a damp shirt. Curl it around to create a design.

Spray (following the manufacturer's instructions) over the top. Then spray another color or two.

Remove the spaghetti carefully. Rinse the shirt in water. Heat set.

Oil Crayon Rubbings

You'll need:
Shiva or Pentel paintsticks
Rubber stamps
Shirt

Examples of various types of paintsticks and rubber stamps.

Hold the shirt over a rubber stamp.

Rub the paintstick over the raised surface of the stamp. Heat set.

Oil Crayon Rubbing using Masking Tape:

Rip pieces of masking tape into thin strips. Stick them onto the shirt, overlapping and forming a design. Rub various colors of paintsticks over the taped area. Remove the tape and heat set.

Sun Printing

You'll need:
Sun Printing Fabric Paint (Seta Colors by Pebeo) or Lumiere paint (Jacquard)
Leaves or other natural material
Foam brush
Piece of glass
Shirt

Dampen the shirt and lay it on your work surface. Paint the shirt using your desired paint and a foam brush.

Lay the natural objects (leaves, ferns, etc.) on the painted shirt and press down firmly.

Place a piece of glass (non UV protectant) over the top to keep flat. Place the arrangement in strong sunlight.

When the fabric is dry, remove the objects and iron the shirt to heat set.

Heat Setting

To make your painted or dyed design permanent, it helps to heat set it. This is done by pressing the garment with a dry iron and pressing cloth.

1. PINK/GREEN "SKIRT"

You will need two tee-shirts the same size in different colors, such as the pink and green shirts pictured.

Green shirt:

1. Cut off the bottom part of the green shirt ¼" down from the sleeves.

2. Cut up the center front.

3. Open up the fabric and lay on a flat surface. Using a plate for a template, place on each end and trace a curved edge (a).

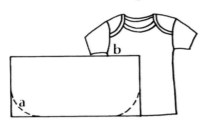

4. Wrap the green shirt around the pink shirt ¼" down from the sleeve seams, matching the side seams and center front (b). Pin in place and topstitch ¼" from the edge.

5. Lettuce (page 49) around the edges of the green shirt and edges of the pink sleeves.

6. Pin ribbon around the top of the green shirt to hide the stitching and topstitch in place.

7. Hand sew on a bow.

2. ROSE PETALS

1. See page 49 for instructions on making a balloon skirt, but before sewing the running stitch in step 5, place the silk rose petals inside the netting. Complete skirt.

2. Pin the skirt around the tee-shirt stretching the shirt as you go and sew in place.

3. Cover the gathers with ribbon and topstitch in place.

4. Cut the sleeves off of the tee-shirt outside the stitch line.

5. Hand sew ribbon and small silk rose to neckline.

3. PINK TUTU

This project is made using two layers of tulle. The bottom layer is a dark pink and the top layer a lighter pink with hearts. The two layers of tulle are cut the same and put together.

1. Follow instructions on page 49 to assemble a skirt or a ruffle.

2. The gathers are encased in decorative seam binding and top-stitched to the tee-shirt.

3. Hand stitch small satin roses across the seam binding.

4. HANKIE DRESS

Six handkerchiefs were used for this shirt (size 3 months). You may need to adjust the amount of hankies needed depending on the size shirt you are using.

The pattern on page 59 works for all sizes of handkerchiefs. The placement on the corners of the handkerchief will vary. It is important to match the dots on the pattern to the edges of the hankie. (see diagram a)

Note: The point of the pattern will not always match the point of the hankie.

1. Lay the pattern on the hankies and cut out (a).

2. With right sides facing, match the side edges together (b), pin and sew using ¼" seam allowance forming a circle with the hankies (c).

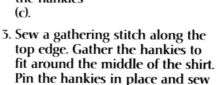

3. Sew a gathering stitch along the top edge. Gather the hankies to fit around the middle of the shirt. Pin the hankies in place and sew to the shirt, stretching the shirt slightly.

4. Pin ribbon around the shirt to hide the gathers and topstitch.

5. Hand sew on a small pink satin rose to the front.

5. LAVENDER CUT-UP

1. With disappearing ink or dress maker's chalk, draw a shape on the front of the shirt 3" x 3½" (a). Adjust this measurement to fit the size of your shirt.

2. Draw vertical lines every ½" within this shape. Cut on the vertical lines.

3. Tie coordinating colors of embroidery floss around these strips in various places (refer to photo, page 6).

4. Cut a piece of fabric (can be from another tee-shirt or a scrap of fabric) in a coordinating color 4½" x 5".

5. On the right side of the fabric, fuse ¼" Steam-A-Seam2 hemming tape around all four edges.

6. Fuse the fabric to the wrong side of the tee-shirt over the cut out area.

Optional: Use the same colors of embroidery floss and blanket stitch around the neck and sleeves.

6. 3-TIERED LETTUCE SLEEVES

To add lettuce edges (see page 49) to each sleeve:

1. Measure the distance from the shoulder seam to where you want the top row of the lettuce edging and mark. Measure down from that mark to position the next row of lettuce edge and mark.

2. Turn the entire sleeve under to the inside, up to the top mark and lettuce along the fold.

3. Repeat Step 2 at second mark.

4. Finish with another lettuce edge along the bottom of each sleeve and along the bottom of the shirt.

Dyeing the shirt:

Note: The shirt will be dyed in three sections. Wear rubber gloves when dyeing this project.

1. Mix the dye in a large bowl or bucket following manufacturer's instructions.

2. Wet the shirt and, holding the shoulders with your fingers, immerse the bottom end of the shirt and sleeves in the dye. Move the fabric up and down with the bottom of the shirt and sleeves remaining submerged until the shirt has a gradated appearance (darker at the bottom, lighter at the top) Remember that it will be lighter when it dries.

3. When you're happy with the effect, rinse the shirt in cold running water until water runs clear.

4. Hang up to dry. Heat set.

7. PINK SHRUG

1. Lay the shirt flat. Measure down 3" under each arm and mark. Draw a horizontal line across the shirt and cut.

2. Place a ruler diagonally across the sleeve starting from the sleeve seam to the top of the sleeve (a). Mark and cut off.

3. Cut up the center front of the shirt.

4. Cut the ribbing off around the neck.

5. Use a bowl or plate for a template to round the front edges of the shrug (b).

6. With excess fabric, cut out two ties (pattern on page 60).

7. Sew one tie on each side of the shrug at the neckline and then tie.

8. GREEN FAUX JACKET

1. Find the center of the tee-shirt (page 49).

2. With the shirt still folded in half, measure in 3/8" from the fold and machine sew down the shirt.

3. Open up the shirt and iron the "flap" to the right side.

4. Use the patterns on page 60 to cut out the faux felt buttons.

5. Put the small circles on the larger circles and sew small circular gathering stitches in the middle to hold them together. Pull thread to gather.

6. Position buttons on the shirt (refer to photo) and hand sew on.

9. PINK SIDE-LACED

1. Cut off the sleeves inside the stitch line, and the ribbing around the neck.

2. Cut ½" slits ½" apart, ¼" in from one side seam, cutting through both front and back of shirt. (see diagram a)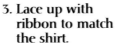

3. Lace up with ribbon to match the shirt.

4. Optional: sew tiny buttons down the front (refer to photo page 8).

10. GREEN TIE AT WAIST

1. Cut bottom band off of shirt. Set aside.

2. Cut slits 1½" in from each side seam and about ¾" long in front and back of shirt.

3. Then cut two more slits about 1¼" in from these two slits.

(Adjust these measurements to fit your particular shirt)

4. Use the bottom band to lace through the slits. Pull it tightly to stretch it out to its full length. Tie in front.

11. ZEBRA PRINT

1. Cut various lengths of animal print and polka dot ribbon into strips. Pin or glue down one side of the shirt.

2. Use a zigzag stitch to secure the strips to the shirt.

3. To add the fur cuffs: Cut off the ribbing around the edge of the sleeve.

4. Measure the circumference of the sleeve and add ½".

5. Decide on the width you want for the cuff and add ¼" to the measurement.

6. Cut a piece of faux fur to that measurement. With right sides facing, sew short ends together using ¼" seam allowance forming a circle.

7. Pin the cuff to the bottom of the sleeve with the right side of the cuff facing the wrong side of the sleeve with edges and seams matching.

8. Sew the cuff on using a ¼" seam allowance. Clip the seam and turn right side out and turn cuff up.

12. ANIMAL PRINT RUFFLES

Dyeing Instructions:

1. Wet the shirt and submerge in black dye. Let soak overnight.

2. When dry, create bunches of fabric and rubber band around each bunch tightly.

3. Soak the shirt in a mixture of bleach and water (1:1). Leave in the bleach mixture for about 10 to 30 minutes. Check to see if the fabric is bleaching. Don't leave in the bleach too long. Bleach may break down the fabric.

4. Rinse the bleach out of the shirt and hang to dry. Heat set.

Ruffle Skirt

1. Make two ruffles following in-structions on page 49.

2. With right sides facing, pin the first ruffle around the bottom of the shirt with edges matching. Sew in place using ¼" seam allowance. Trim seam and press the ruffle down.

3. With right sides facing, pin the second ruffle onto the tee-shirt with the gathered edge ½" from the first ruffle. Sew in place along gathers. Trim the seam and iron the ruffle down over the first ruffle.

13. STRIPED CARDIGAN

1. Find the center of the shirt (see page 49). Open up the shirt and cut up the fold line. Turn back raw edges ½" and sew.

2. To make the fabric pockets, cut two pieces of coordinating print fabrics 4½" x 5¼" for a 4" x 4¼" pocket. (Adjust the measurement to fit your shirt.)

3. Turn the sides and bottom of the pockets under ¼" and press with an iron.

4. Fold the top of the pocket under ½" and press.

5. Position the pockets on the shirt (refer to photo for placement). Pin in place and topstitch along the sides and bottom.

14. DIAMOND CUT

1. With disap–pearing ink or dress maker's chalk, draw diamond shapes on shirt (pattern on page 60).

2. Draw vertical lines every ½" across these diamonds as shown on pattern.

3. Cut on these vertical lines.

4. Cut 3½" squares of fabric. Use a patterned fabric with colors that coordinate with the tee–shirt.

5. On the right side of the fabric pieces, fuse ¼" Steam–a–Seam2 hemming tape around all four edges.

6. Fuse the fabric to the wrong side of the tee–shirt over the cut out area.

7. Pull the edges of the strips to stretch them so that more fabric shows through the openings.

15. PURPLE TIES
(use a larger size shirt)

1. Cut off the neck ribbing of the tee–shirt.

2. Cut shirt up the middle (see page 49).

3. Cut strips about 2" long evenly spaced about 1" apart. (Adjust this to fit the size of your shirt.)

4. Tie the strips together. (When dressing baby, just untie the first few strips.)

16. PINK WITH TIE

1. Cut neckband, sleeves and bottom band off of the shirt (a). Retain one sleeve.

2. Cut a small slit in the center front of the shirt, down 1" from the neckline (b).

3. Cut the sleeve open. Lay it flat and cut from the center of the straight edge out to each edge to form the tie (c).

4. Thread the tie through the slit and tie into a knot (d).

18. YELLOW WITH RUFFLES

Recycle parts of the tee–shirts your baby has outgrown to create this style of shirt.

1. Cut the hems off of two tee–shirts (preferably different colors) above the stitching line.

2. Measure down ⅛" or ¼" (depending on the width of the hem) from the top and sew a gathering stitch.

3. Gather the band to form a ruffle and fit across the front of the shirt.

4. Pin the first ruffle to the shirt 1" down from the sleeve seams with the gathered edge toward the bottom of the shirt. Sew along the gather line.

5. Position the second ruffle ¼" below the first, again with the gathered edge toward the bottom of the shirt. Sew in place.

6. Trim close to the stitching. Turn the ruffles facing down and press with an iron.

7. Measure around the bottom of the sleeve. Cut two pieces of round cord elastic to that measurement, plus 1".

8. Thread the cord on the inside of each sleeve through the hem stitching using a large eye needle.

9. Pull the ends together slightly gathering the sleeves. Overlap the ends (trim if necessary) and machine stitch back and forth across to secure.

10. Measure around the neck and repeat steps 8 and 9.

19. CLEVER POCKET

1. Turn the onesie over and cut across about 5" up from the crotch (a). Then cut across the crotch (b).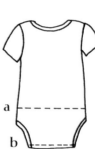

2. Discard the front piece with the snaps. Turn the other piece right side up and position it at the bottom of the front of the shirt (c).

3. Topstitch each side with a double seam, leaving the pocket areas open.

4. Topstitch across the top of the pocket also with a double seam.

5. Topstitch across the bottom of the pocket with a double seam.

20. YELLOW SHRUG

1. Follow instructions on page 55 for Pink Shrug for cutting the tee–shirt.

2. Cut the ribbing off of the sleeves.

3. Sew on rickrack around each sleeve and around the front and bottom of the shrug. Start at the neckline on one side and end at the bottom center back. Repeat on the opposite side ending at the center back and tucking the end of the rickrack under for a finished look.

22. PATCHWORK RUFFLE

1. Stretch the bottom of the shirt slightly and measure the circumference.

2. Decide on the number of squares for your ruffle. Divide the number of squares into the above measurement and add 2½" to each square for the length. For the width of each square, add 1" to the finished size. Cut out the squares to those measurements.

3. With right sides facing, sew the short ends of the squares together using ¼" seam allowance forming a circle.

4. Machine hem one long side of the circle turning the edge under ¼" and then another ¼".

5. Sew a gathering stitch ¼" down from the edge of the opposite side. Pull the threads to fit the bottom of the shirt, stretching the shirt bottom.

6. With right sides together and edges matching, pin the ruffle to the shirt bottom positioning squares and adjusting gathers.

7. Sew the ruffle onto the shirt using ½" seam allowance. Trim seam.

23. TRI-COLOR DIAGONAL

Dyeing:

1. Use three different bowls and mix the dye in each (following manufacturer's instructions).

2. Dip one sleeve in the dye for about 10 minutes. Dip the other sleeve in the second color.

3. Wrap plastic baggies around each dyed sleeve and wrap tightly with rubber bands.

4. Submerge the shirt in the third bowl of dye and let soak for about 30 minutes.

5. Remove the shirt from the dye. Remove the baggies. Rinse the shirt under cold running water until the water runs clear. Hang to dry.

Cutting:

1. Lay a ruler diagonally across the bottom of the shirt starting from the lower right hand corner. Adjust the degree of the cut by moving the ruler up or down on the left. Draw a line along the edge of the ruler for a guide and then cut the bottom off the shirt.

2. Stitch a lettuce edge (see page 49) around the bottom, neck and sleeves of the shirt.

25. POCKET TIE-DYE

You will need:
    3 colors of dye
    3 applicator bottles with tips

1. Prepare three colors of dye and fill the applicator bottles.

2. With the shirt still damp, fan fold it lengthwise. Wrap rubber bands around the folds about every 2".

3. Apply the different colors of dye using the applicator bottles, squirting randomly over the shirt and into the folds.

4. Place shirt in a baggie and let sit over night.

5. Clip off the rubber bands and run the shirt under cold water until the water runs clear. Hang to dry. Heat set.

6. Cut off the sleeves along inside seam line. Discard one. Lay the sleeve flat with the seam center back and top edges matching. Pin to shirt with rounded edge at bottom. Topstitch sides with ¼" seams. Topstitch bottom along existing seam line.

26. SUNBURST

You will need:
    4 – 5 colors of dye
    4 – 5 applicator bottles with tips

1. Prepare 4 to 5 colors of dye such as red, blue, green, orange and purple. Fill applicator bottles with the dye.

2. Grab the center front of the damp onesie and pull to form a cone. Wrap rubber bands starting at the smallest end of the "cone" and continue wrapping rubber bands about every 2".

3. Apply first color of dye to smallest part of the cone, then second, third and so on.

4. Squirt each dye color in between all folds so that all parts of the shirt are dyed.

5. Place shirt in plastic baggie and let sit over night.

6. Remove rubber bands. Run shirt under cold water until water runs clear. Hang to dry. Heat set.

27. FLOWER TIE-DYE

1. Prepare blue and green dye in separate bowls.

2. While the shirt is still damp, fold it lengthwise with a fan fold. Wrap rubber bands around evenly about every 2". Include the sleeves in the folds.

3. Place in the green dye and soak for about 45 minutes.

4. Remove from dye and clip off rubber bands. Run under cold water until water runs clear.

5. Then fanfold the shirt widthwise and wrap with rubber bands as in step 2.

6. Place in blue dye for 45 minutes and repeat Step 4. Hang to dry. Heat set.

7. Use the pattern on page 61 for the flower design. Fuse the flower to the shirt following the fusing instructions on page 50.

44. RED/GREEN FLOWERS

1. Prepare red and green dye in separate bowls.

2. Dip bottom 3" of the damp shirt in red and let soak for 45 minutes.

3. Dip remainder in green with the red part outside of the bowl. Let soak in the dye for 45 minutes.

4. Run under cold water until water runs clear. Hang to dry. Heat set.

5. Cut designs from a floral print fabric. Follow the fusing instructions (page 50) and iron them to the shirt.

6. Add embroidery stitches following the details of the design.

52. FISH

1. Prepare blue and green dye in separate bowls.

2. Dip ⅓ of the damp onesie in the green dye. Leave for 45 minutes.

3. Dip the center of the shirt in the blue dye for 45 minutes leaving the other ends of the onesie outside of the bowl.

4. Dip the last ⅓ in green for 45 minutes.

5. Run under cold water until water runs clear. Hang to dry. Heat set.

6. Use the pattern on page 67 for the fish design.

7. Follow fusing instructions on page 50 to apply the fish and bubbles to the shirt.

8. If desired, use a blanket stitch to secure the appliqué to the shirt. See stitch instructions page 51.

68. NEW BLUE SLEEVES

1. Cut the sleeves off the shirt outside the seams.

2. Measure the circumference of the armhole and add 2".

3. To make a pattern for the new sleeves: On a piece of tracing paper, draw a line the length of the measurement just taken.

4. Find the center of the line and measure up 3" and mark.

5. Draw a crescent shape the length of the line (a).

6. Pin the pattern to the fabric and cut out two pieces.

7. Turn the straight edge under ¼" and sew.

8. With right sides together, fold each piece in half and sew points together (b). Mark the top of the fold line.

9. Sew a gathering stitch along the crescent side (c) of the sleeve ¼" in from the edge. Pull threads to gather evenly around the sleeve.

10. With right sides facing and edges matching, pin the seam of the sleeve to the side seam of the shirt, and the fold mark to the shoulder seam (d). Adjust gathers to fit and sew in place with ¼" seam allowance (e). Trim seams. Fold out sleeve and press.

80. ARGYLE

1. Cut out the neck and sleeves as shown in diagram.

2. Position the pattern on the shirt and trace.

3. Cut out the diamond shapes from burgundy felt. Fuse them in position on the shirt.

4. Embroider with a running stitch and 2 strands of black embroidery floss.

85. PAINT STICK STRIPES

1. Place strips of masking tape on the white shirt. Follow the photo on page 38 or try your own design.

2. Color over the shirt and the tape using different shades of Shiva Paintsticks (see page 53).

3. When finished, remove the tape and heat set.

86. PAINT STICK ANCHOR

1. Place a rubber stamp under the top layer of the shirt (see page 53).

2. Carefully color over the top of the stamp with Shiva Paintsticks as if you're doing a rubbing.

3. Add the wavy design in the same manner using another stamp.

4. When finished, add blanket stitching to the collar, sleeves and bottom edge using matching colors of floss (page 51).

88. NATURE

1. Use a foam brush to apply paint (we used Seta Colors) to a damp shirt. See page 53.

2. Lay leaves randomly on the shirt (flat ones work best).

3. Place a square of glass over the top to keep leaves in place and set the shirt in the sun for about an hour. The sun will do the rest.

4. Remove the glass and leaves.

89. ROCK STAR

Dyeing instructions:

1. Prepare blue dye according to manufacturer's instructions.

2. Fanfold a green onesie widthwise (a).

3. Wrap a rubber band on only the left side of the folded onesie (b). Fanfold the sleeves and wrap rubber bands in 2 or 3 places.

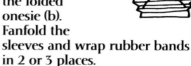

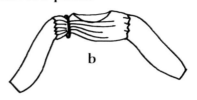

4. Soak the shirt in dye for 45 minutes.

5. Remove rubber bands.

6. Run under cold water until water runs clear. Hang to dry. Heat set.

7. Use alphabet stamps and fabric paint in your desired color to add "Rock Star" to the shirt.

92. RICKRACK JACKET

1. Find the center of the shirt (see page 49). Open up the shirt and cut up the fold line.

2. Cut the ribbing off of the sleeves and the bottom of the shirt.

3. Sew jumbo rickrack along the front edge and the bottom edge of the shirt.

4. Start adding the rickrack at the neckline on one side and end at the bottom center back. Repeat on the opposite side ending at the center back and tucking the end of the rickrack under for a finished look.

5. Position and glue the other rickrack diagonally on the shirt (refer to photo page 41). Tuck ends under at each end and glue to hold in place. Machine-sew rickrack down.

6. Add lettuce edges to the sleeves (see page 49).

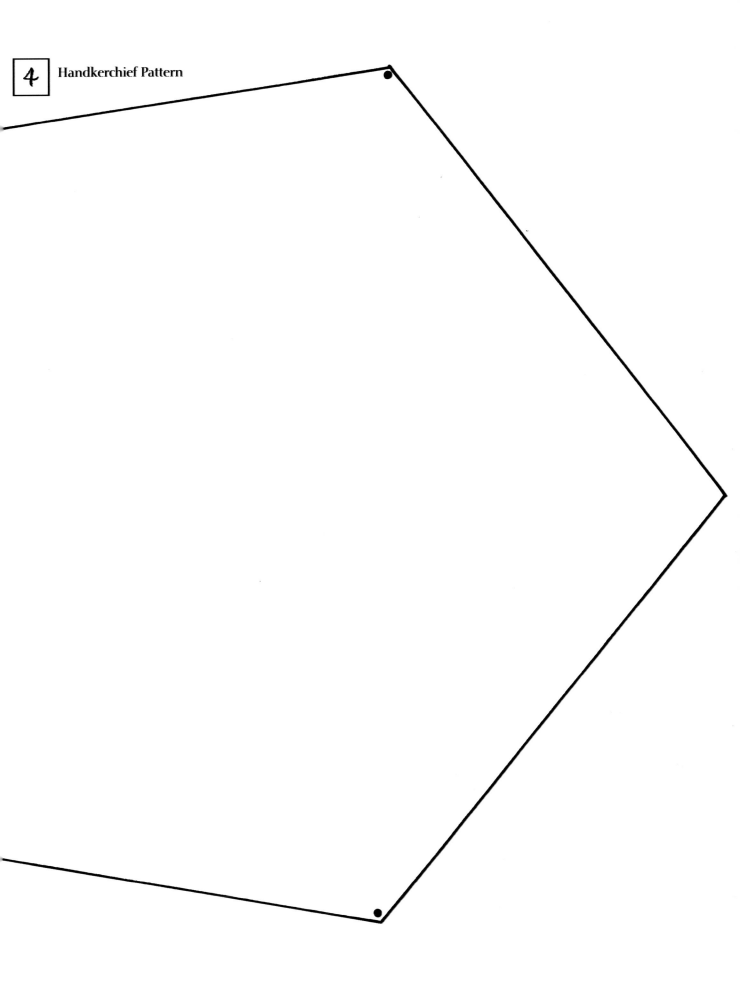

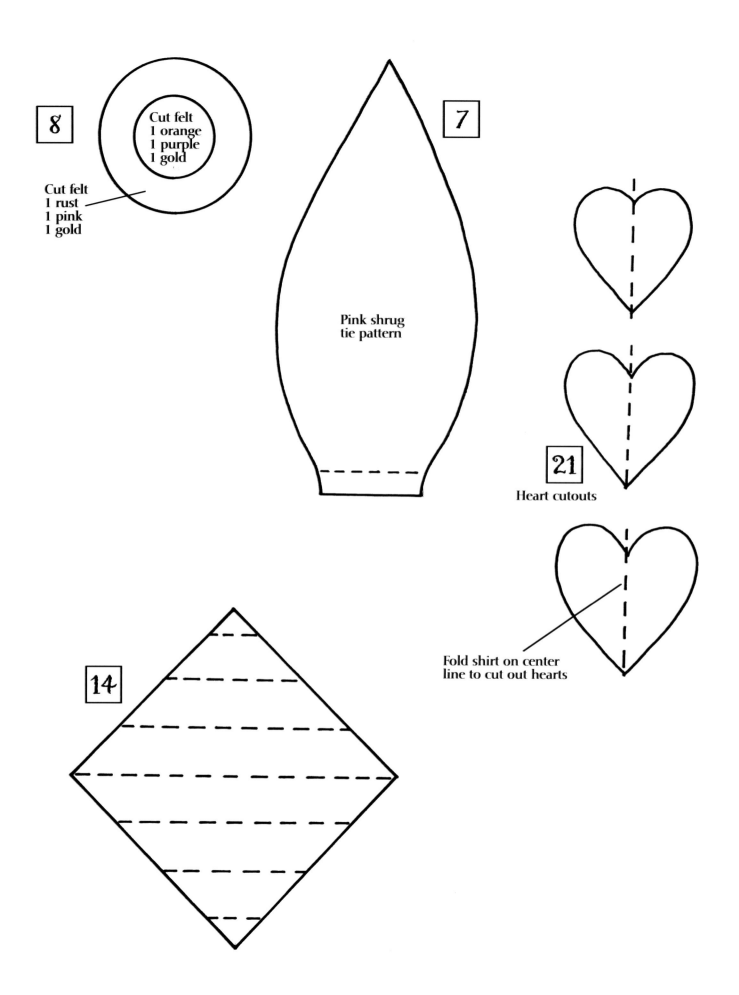

8

Cut felt
1 orange
1 purple
1 gold

Cut felt
1 rust
1 pink
1 gold

7

Pink shrug
tie pattern

21

Heart cutouts

Fold shirt on center
line to cut out hearts

14

French knot

Lavender
lazy daisy

k
y
sy

Turquoise
lazy daisy

(three strands)

Green
lazy
daisy

en
y
sy

1/8"
green
ribbon

1/8"
green
ribbon

1/8"
green
ribbon

r
en
on

Lavender
backstitch

Green lazy
daisies

Red
backstitch

Orange
backstitch

French
knots

Green

Green

Green
lazy
daisies

Green

Gold

Orange

Green

Green

Lavender

(all two strands)

28

29

27

Blue fleece

Green fleece

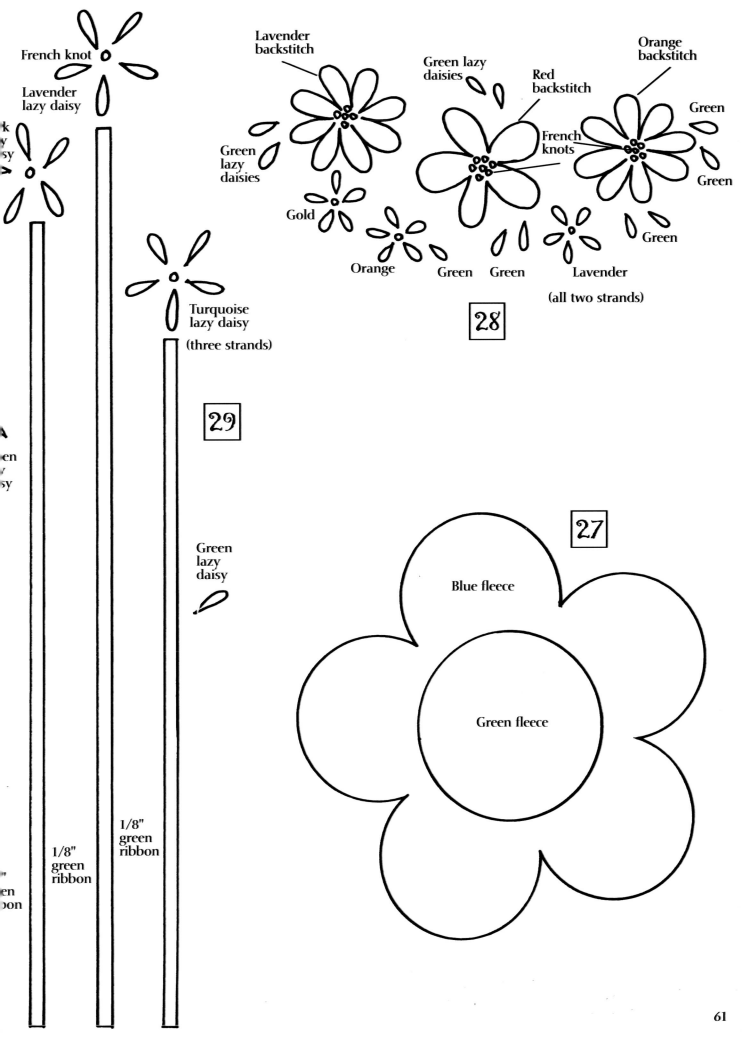

30 Little ♥ Love

Lavender backstitch (two strands)

32 White french knots

Black (eyes)

Black french knot

White satin stitch

White satin stitch

31 Paris

Black backstitch (one strand)

33 Silver

Silver

Princess

Silver

Silver

Silver

Silver

Silver

Silver

Lavender backstitch (one strand)

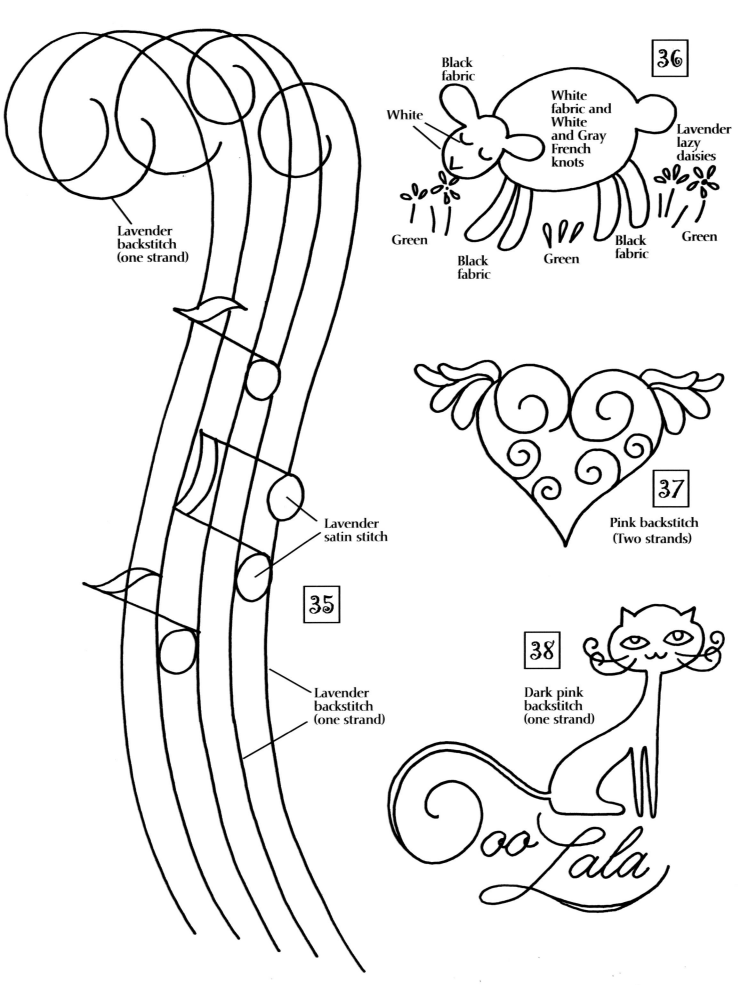

Lavender
backstitch
(one strand)

Lavender
satin stitch

35

Lavender
backstitch
(one strand)

36

Black
fabric

White

White
fabric and
White
and Gray
French
knots

Lavender
lazy
daisies

Green

Black
fabric

Green

Black
fabric

Green

37

Pink backstitch
(Two strands)

38

Dark pink
backstitch
(one strand)

Ooo Lala

63

34

Chain Stitches
(two strands)

DMC colors used:
Lt. Tan 437
Copper 920
Coral 893
Sand 3773
Lt. Avocado 471
Gray Green 926
Sky Blue 519

39

Pink
satin
stitch
(two strands)

Kiss Me

Black backstitch (one strand)

42

Sweet Pea

Green backstitch
(two strands)

(three strands)

Large Pink
French knots

Large
Dark
Pink
French
knots

41

40

Green
backstitch
(two strands)

Green
French
knots

Green chain stitch
and veins backstitched

(three strands)

64

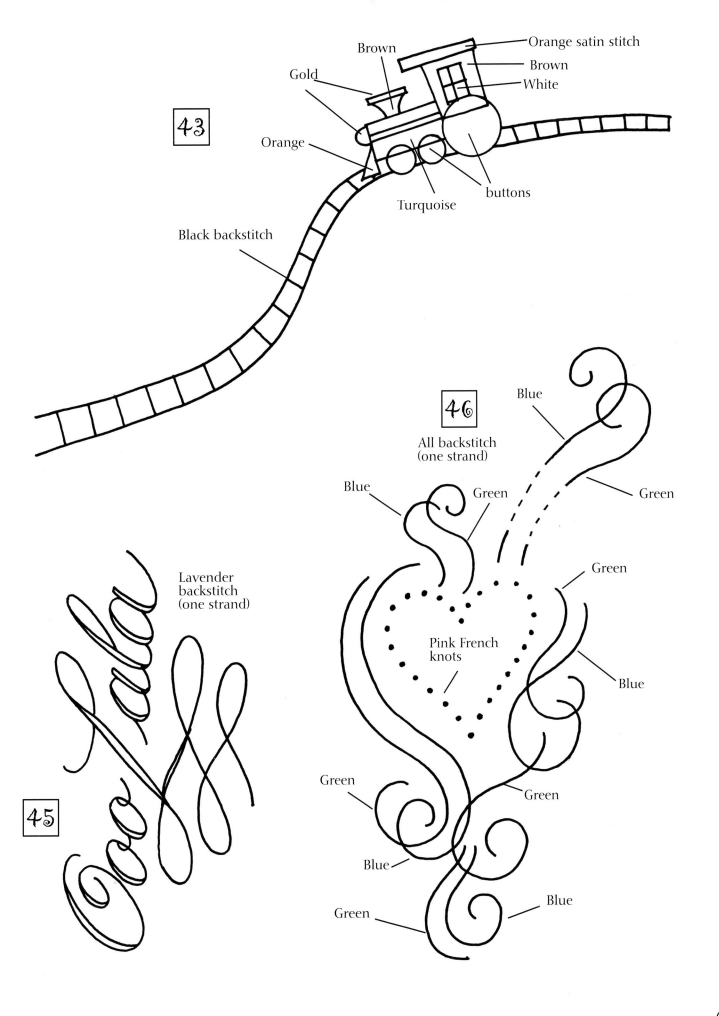

Brown

Orange satin stitch

Gold

Brown

White

43

Orange

Turquoise

buttons

Black backstitch

46

Blue

All backstitch
(one strand)

Blue

Green

Green

Green

Lavender
backstitch
(one strand)

Blue

Pink French
knots

Green

Green

45

Green

Blue

Blue

Green

Blue

47

Periwinkle
backstitch
(three strands)

47

Green
lazy
daisies
(three strands)

Lavender
lazy daisies
(three strands)

Blue lazy
daisies
(three strands)

Green
backstitch
(two strands)

French
knot

48

Periwinkle
backstitch
(three strands)

Green
lazy
daisies
(three strands)

Pink
lazy
daisies
(three strands)

Green
backstitch
(two strands)

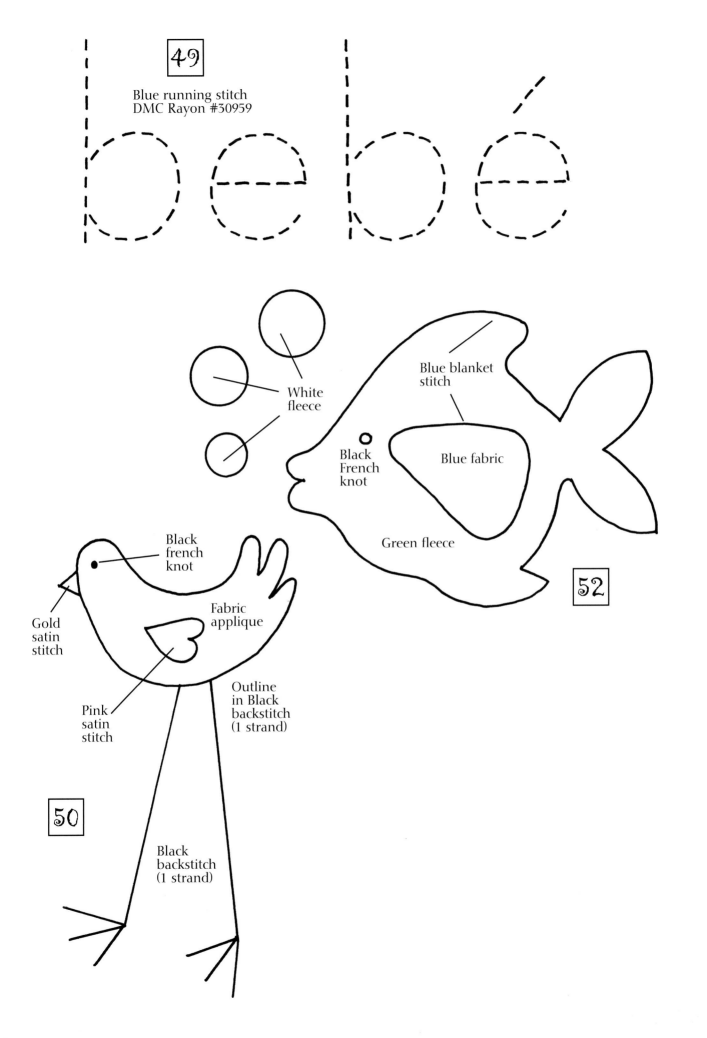

49

Blue running stitch
DMC Rayon #30959

bebé

White
fleece

Blue blanket
stitch

Black
French
knot

Blue fabric

Green fleece

52

Black
french
knot

Fabric
applique

Gold
satin
stitch

Pink
satin
stitch

Outline
in Black
backstitch
(1 strand)

50

Black
backstitch
(1 strand)

67

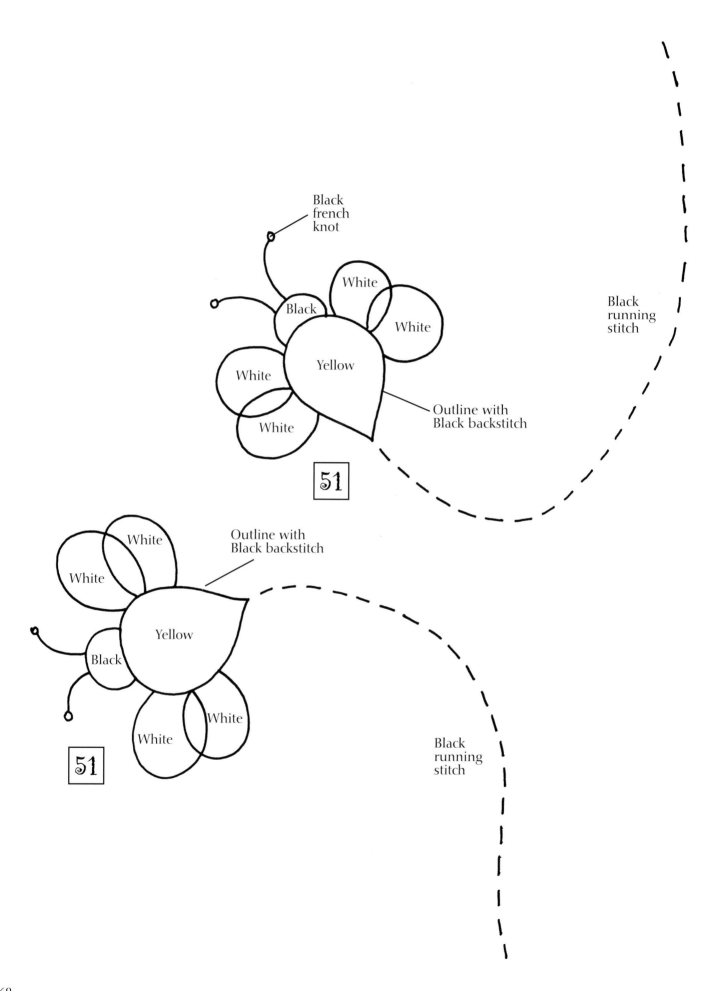

Black
french
knot

White

Black

White

White

Yellow

Outline with
Black backstitch

Black
running
stitch

51

Outline with
Black backstitch

White

White

Yellow

Black

White

White

Black
running
stitch

51

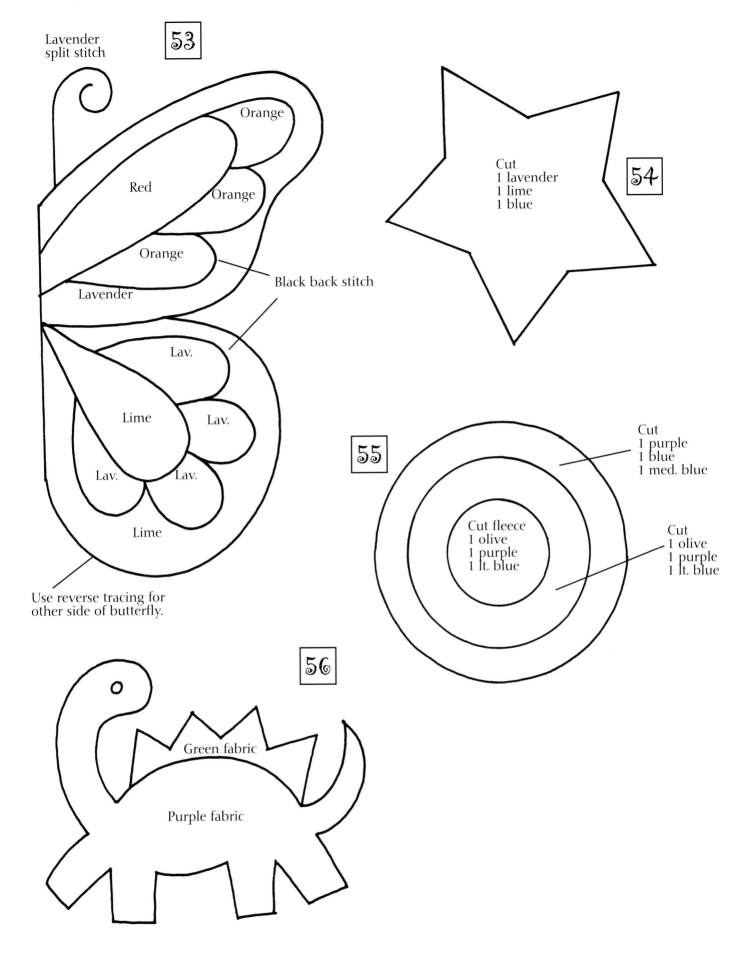

Lavender
split stitch

53

Orange

Red

Orange

Orange

Lavender

Black back stitch

Lav.

Lime

Lav.

Lav.

Lav.

Lime

Use reverse tracing for
other side of butterfly.

54

Cut
1 lavender
1 lime
1 blue

55

Cut
1 purple
1 blue
1 med. blue

Cut fleece
1 olive
1 purple
1 lt. blue

Cut
1 olive
1 purple
1 lt. blue

56

Green fabric

Purple fabric

57

Black

Gold

Lime
Green

White

58

See photo for
fabric suggestions

Black
satin
stitch

59

Black satin stitch
(eyes & nose)

Black
straight
stitch

Purple fabric

Yarn or
cord

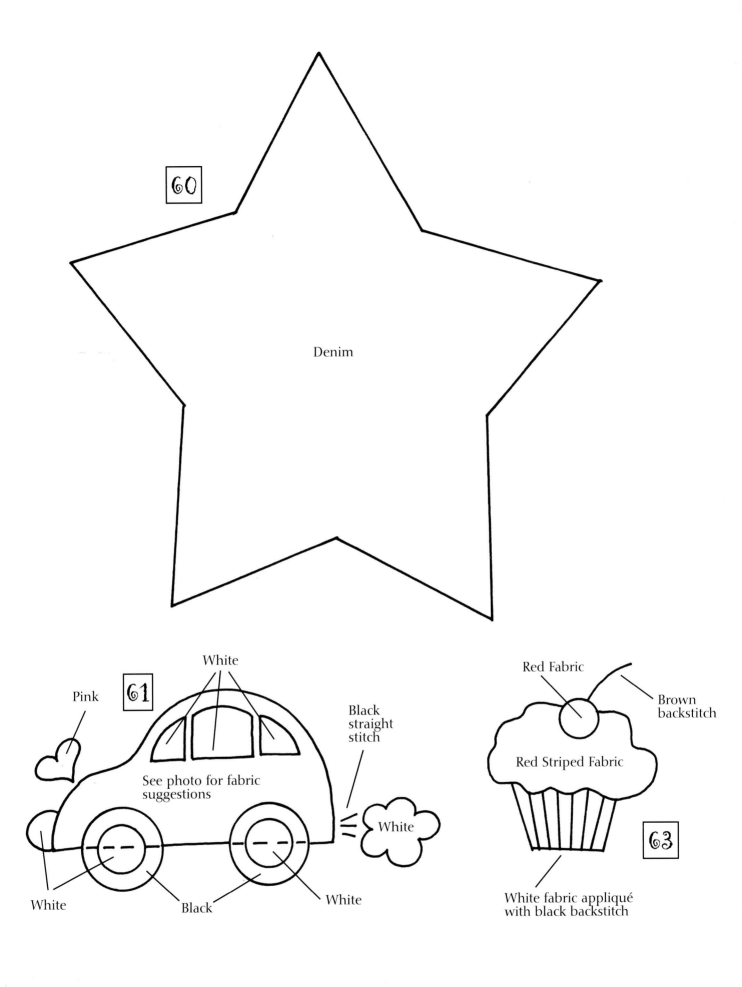

60 Denim

Pink

61 White

See photo for fabric suggestions

Black straight stitch

White

White

Black

White

Red Fabric

Brown backstitch

Red Striped Fabric

63

White fabric appliqué with black backstitch

71

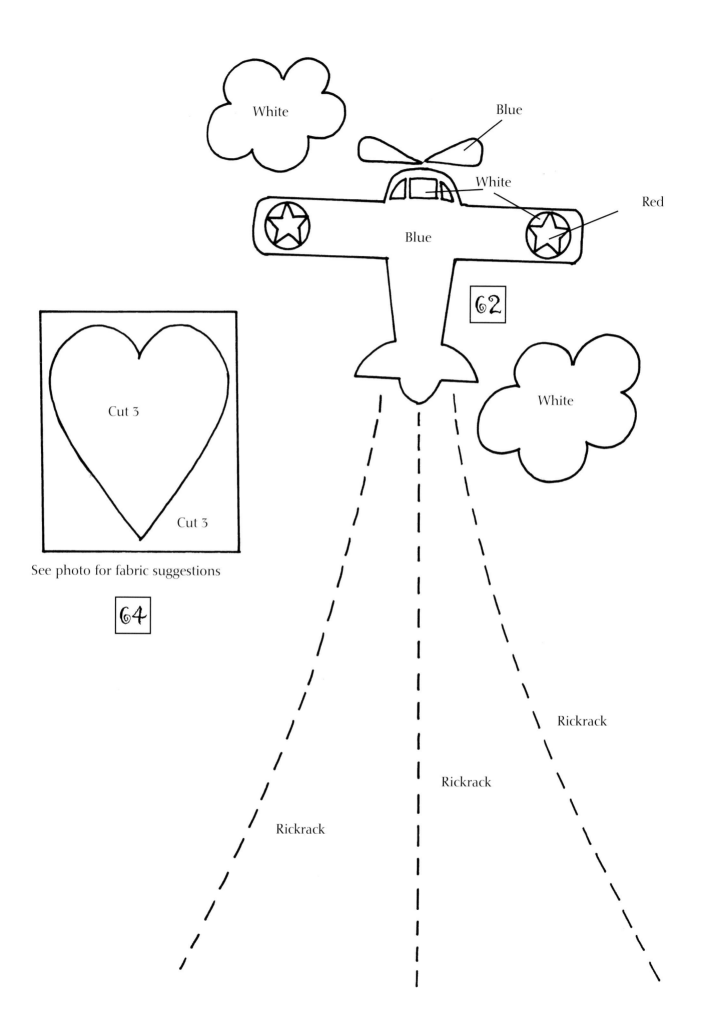

White

Blue

White

Red

Blue

62

Cut 3

Cut 3

See photo for fabric suggestions

64

White

Rickrack

Rickrack

Rickrack

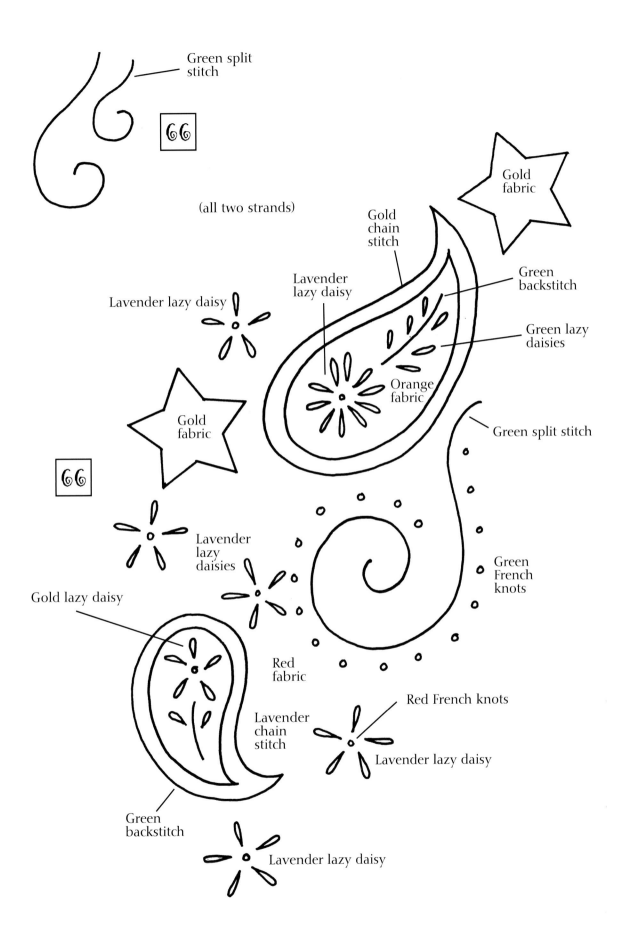

Green split
stitch

66

(all two strands)

Gold
chain
stitch

Lavender
lazy daisy

Gold
fabric

Green
backstitch

Green lazy
daisies

Lavender lazy daisy

Gold
fabric

Orange
fabric

Green split stitch

66

Lavender
lazy
daisies

Green
French
knots

Gold lazy daisy

Red
fabric

Red French knots

Lavender
chain
stitch

Lavender lazy daisy

Green
backstitch

Lavender lazy daisy

Blue

Red

Green
running
stitch

67

Lavender
running
stitch

Yellow

Red

Red
running
stitch

Yellow

Blue

Turquoise
running
stitch

Blue print fabric

68

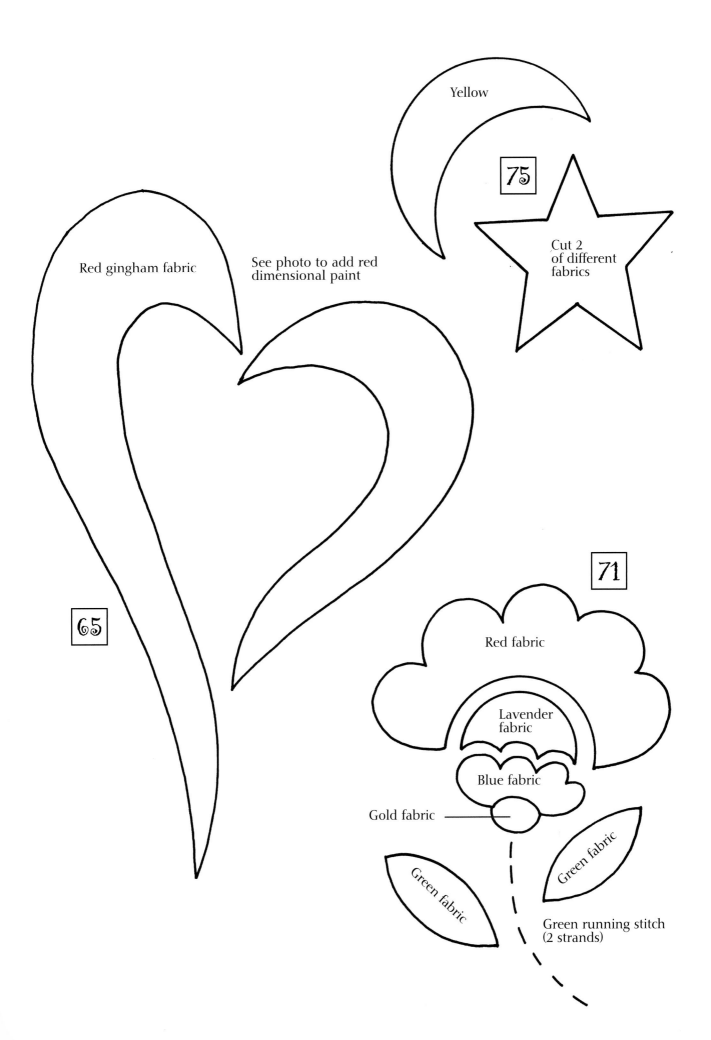

Yellow

75

Cut 2
of different
fabrics

Red gingham fabric

See photo to add red
dimensional paint

65

71

Red fabric

Lavender
fabric

Blue fabric

Gold fabric

Green fabric

Green fabric

Green running stitch
(2 strands)

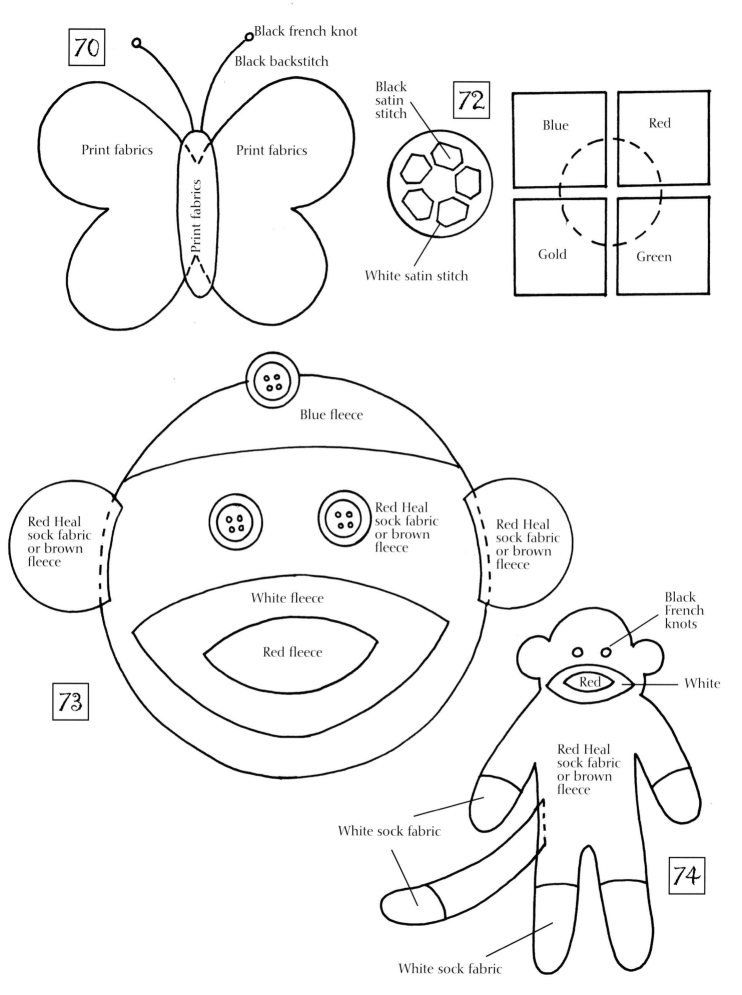

70

Black french knot

Black backstitch

Print fabrics

Print fabrics

Print fabrics

72

Black satin stitch

White satin stitch

Blue

Red

Gold

Green

Blue fleece

Red Heal sock fabric or brown fleece

Red Heal sock fabric or brown fleece

Red Heal sock fabric or brown fleece

White fleece

Red fleece

73

Black French knots

Red

White

Red Heal sock fabric or brown fleece

White sock fabric

74

White sock fabric

76

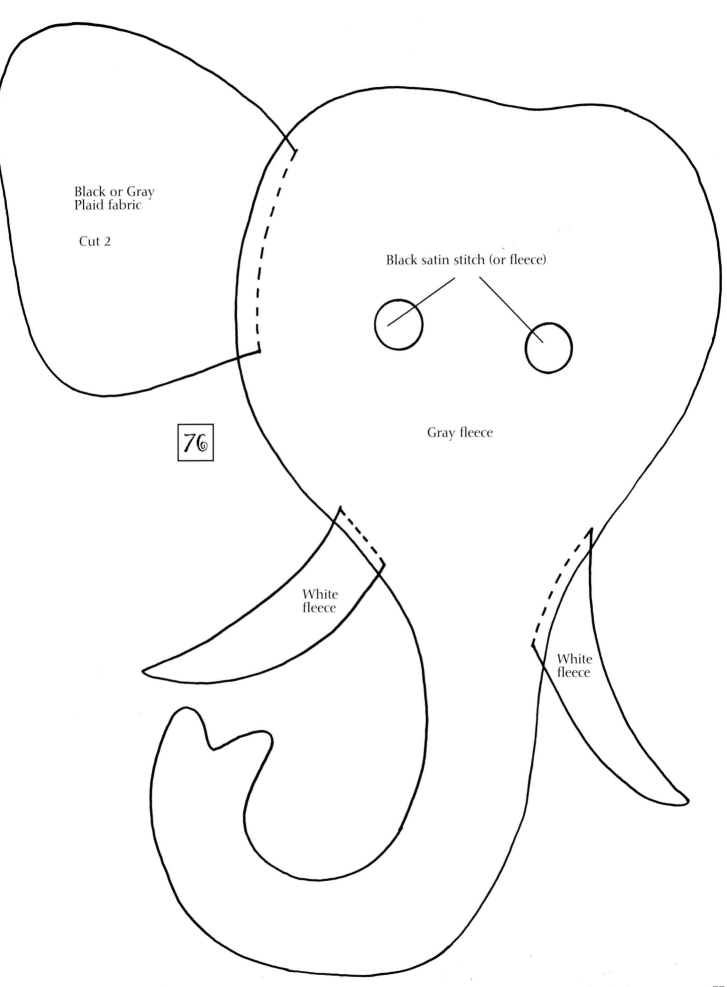

Black or Gray
Plaid fabric

Cut 2

Black satin stitch (or fleece)

76

Gray fleece

White
fleece

White
fleece

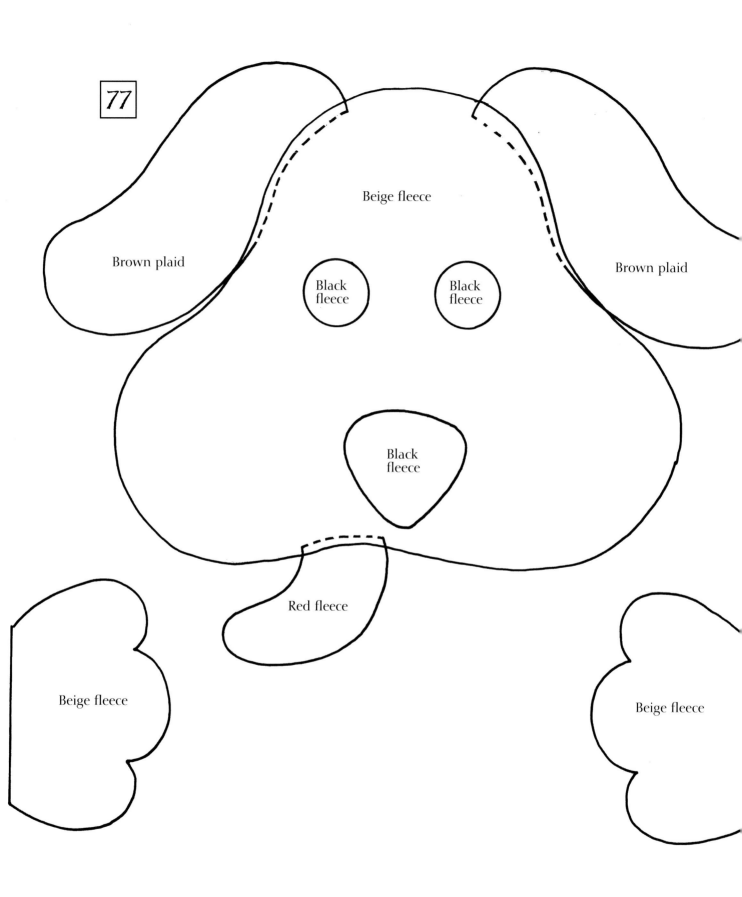

77

Beige fleece

Brown plaid

Brown plaid

Black
fleece

Black
fleece

Black
fleece

Red fleece

Beige fleece

Beige fleece

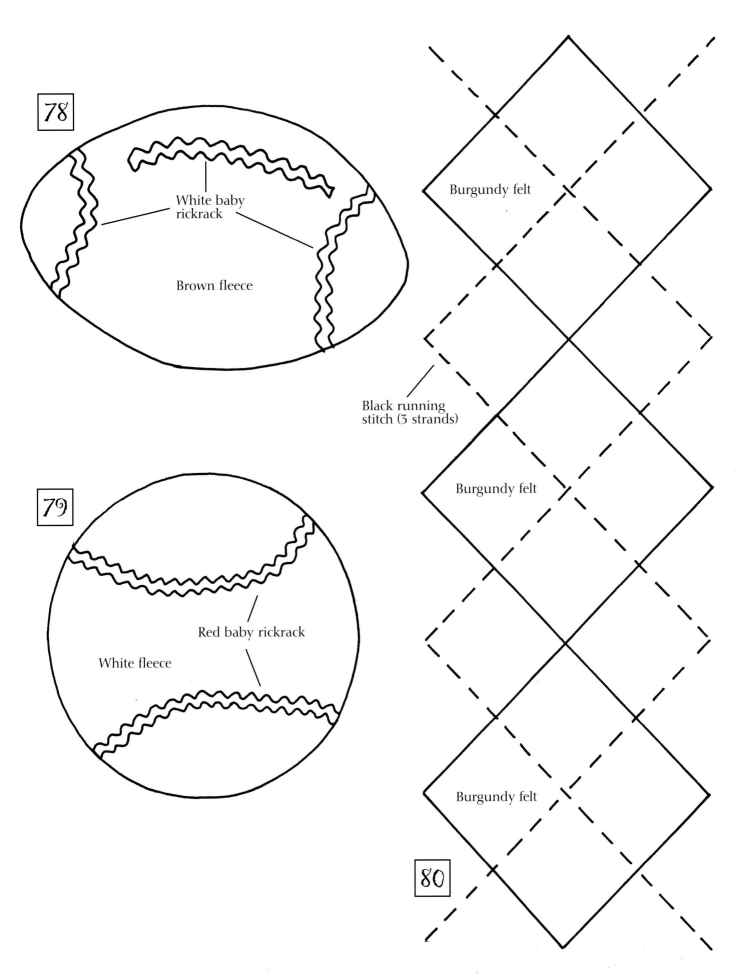

78

White baby
rickrack

Brown fleece

79

Red baby rickrack

White fleece

Burgundy felt

Black running
stitch (3 strands)

Burgundy felt

Burgundy felt

80

Blanket stitch

81

See photo
for fabric
suggestions

Gold

Green

Brown

93